Study Guide

for use with

Fundamental Managerial Accounting Concepts

Thomas P. Edmonds
University of Alabama—Birmingham

Cindy D. Edmonds
University of Alabama—Birmingham

Bor-Yi Tsay
University of Alabama—Birmingham

David E. Eliason
Southern Alberta Institute of Technology

Prepared by
Cindy D. Edmonds
University of Alabama—Birmingham

Philip R. Olds
Virginia Commonwealth University

Michael L. Hockenstein
Vanier College

Boston   Burr Ridge, IL   Dubuque, IA   Madison, WI   New York   San Francisco   St. Louis
Bangkok   Bogotá   Caracas   Lisbon   London   Madrid
Mexico City   Milan   New Delhi   Seoul   Singapore   Sydney   Taipei   Toronto

*McGraw-Hill
Ryerson Limited*

A Subsidiary of The **McGraw-Hill** Companies

**Study Guide for use with
Fundamental Managerial Accounting Concepts
First Canadian Edition**

Copyright © 2003 by McGraw-Hill Ryerson Limited, a Subsidiary of The McGraw-Hill Companies. All rights reserved. No part of this publication may be reproduced or transmitted in any form or by any means, or stored in a data base or retrieval system, without the prior written permission of McGraw-Hill Ryerson Limited, or in the case of photocopying or other reprographic copying, a license from CANCOPY (the Canadian Copyright Licensing Agency), 6 Adelaide Street East, Suite 900, Toronto, Ontario, M5C 1H6.

Any request for photocopying, recording, or taping of any part of this publication shall be directed in writing to CANCOPY.

ISBN: 0-07-091492-3

1 2 3 4 5 6 7 8 9 10 CP 0 9 8 7 6 5 4 3

Printed and bound in Canada

Care has been taken to trace ownership of copyright material contained in this text; however, the publisher will welcome any information that enables them to rectify any reference or credit for subsequent editions.

Executive Editor: Nicole Lukach
Sponsoring Editor: Lenore Gray Spence
Developmental Editor: Katherine Goodes
Director of Marketing: Jeff MacLean
Production Coordinator: Andree Davis
Cover Design: Greg Devitt
Printer: Canadian Printco

TABLE OF CONTENTS

CHAPTER 1	1
CHAPTER 2	23
CHAPTER 3	41
CHAPTER 4	57
CHAPTER 5	74
CHAPTER 6	92
CHAPTER 7	108
CHAPTER 8	126
CHAPTER 9	142
CHAPTER 10	161
CHAPTER 11	180
CHAPTER 12	200
CHAPTER 13	214
CHAPTER 14	231

Chapter 1
Management Accounting: A Value-Added Discipline

Learning Objectives for the Chapter

The material in this chapter of the Study Guide is designed to facilitate your ability to:

- Distinguish between managerial and financial accounting.
- Identify the components of the cost of a product made by a manufacturing company including the cost of materials, labour, and overhead.
- Understand the need to determine the average cost per unit of a product.
- Understand the difference between a cost and an expense.
- Explain how product versus general, selling, and administrative cost affect financial statements.
- Understand how cost classification affects financial statements and managerial decisions.
- Appreciate the need for a code of ethical conduct.
- Distinguish product costs from upstream and downstream cost.
- Understand how products provided by service companies differ from products made by manufacturing companies.
- Explain how emerging trends including activity-based management, value-added assessment, and just-in-time inventory are affecting the managerial accounting discipline.

Brief Explanation of the Learning Objectives

Distinguish between managerial and financial accounting.

Managerial accounting focuses on information that is used for internal decision-making. In contrast, financial accounting focuses on information that is used by investors, creditors, and other interested parties that operate outside the accounting entity. A summary of the key differences between managerial and financial accounting is provided in Exhibit 1-2 of the textbook.

Identify the components of the cost of a product made by a manufacturing company including the cost of materials, labour, and overhead.

The cost of products made by a manufacturing company include direct raw materials, direct labour, and indirect manufacturing costs which are called overhead. Examples, of product costs are shown in Exhibit 1-11 of the textbook.

Understand the need to determine the average cost per unit of a product.

Determining the exact cost of each unit of product made by a company would require an unreasonable amount of record keeping. Indeed, determining the exact cost is virtually impossible. Minute details such as a millisecond of labour cannot be effectively measured. Even if we could determine the exact cost of each table, the information would be of little use. Minor differences in the cost per unit would make no difference in terms of pricing or other decisions that management needs to make. For these reasons, accountants normally calculate cost per unit as an average. The average cost per unit is determined as follows:

Total Cost ÷ Total Units = Average Cost Per Unit

Understand the difference between a cost and an expense.

A cost can be accumulated in an asset account before it is expensed. For example, wages of production workers are accumulated in an inventory account before being expensed as cost of goods sold. A cost can also be expensed directly to the income statement. For example, salaries of sales or administrative staff are expensed immediately.

Explain how product versus general, selling, and administrative cost affect financial statements.

Product costs including the cost of direct materials, direct labour, and overhead are first accumulated in an inventory account and then expensed as cost of goods sold at the time the inventory is sold. Product costs of goods that have not been sold will appear on the balance sheet while product cost of goods sold will appear on the income statement. Many GS&A costs such as salaries and rent are expensed immediately. However, GS&A costs of long-term assets such as office equipment are accumulated in an asset account and expensed in the period that the asset is used.

Understand how cost classification affects financial statements and managerial decisions.

Managers can delay the recognition of expenses by accumulating costs in asset accounts. Delaying the recognition of expense acts to increase the amount of total assets and amount of reported net income. Accordingly, delaying expense recognition provides a more favorable portrayal of a company's financial condition. In addition, managers who receive a bonus that is based on net income benefit when expense recognition is delayed. Since the delay of expense recognition act to increase net income, it will also act to increase income taxes.

Appreciate the need for a code of ethical conduct.

Accountants provide information that is useful for decision-making. If they are not trustworthy, the value of the information they provide is worthless. To secure their value, accountants must abide by a strict code of ethical conduct.

Distinguish product costs from upstream and downstream cost.

Product costs are the costs incurred during the manufacturing process. Most companies incur product-related costs before and after the manufacturing process. Costs that are incurred before the manufacturing process begins are called upstream costs. Examples of upstream costs include research and development costs. Costs that are incurred after the manufacturing process is complete are called downstream costs. Examples of downstream costs include transportation costs, advertising, sales commissions, and bad debts. Profitability analysis requires attention to upstream and downstream costs as well as manufacturing product costs. To be profitable, a company must recover the total cost of developing, producing, and delivering its products to its customers.

Understand how products provided by service companies differ from products made by manufacturing companies.

Service companies, like manufacturing companies, incur materials, labour, and overhead costs in the process of providing services to their customers. The primary difference between manufacturing entities and service companies is that the products provided by service companies are consumed immediately. Accordingly, service companies normally do not accumulate product costs in an inventory account. Instead, product costs of services companies are usually expensed as they are incurred.

Explain how emerging trends including activity-based management, value-added assessment, and just-in-time inventory are affecting the managerial accounting discipline.

Business organization face global competition. In a effort to improve efficiency and effectiveness, companies are demanding that accountants take a more active role in decision-making. Accountants are expected to develop strategies and procedures to more accurately measure and reduce costs, and to identify and eliminate activities that do not add value to the business.

Self-Study Problems

Multiple Choice Problems

1. Which of the following is a characteristic of managerial accounting?
   a. Users of the data are insiders such an managers and employees
   b. Includes physical information about subunits of an organization
   c. Is regulated only by the cost / benefit rule
   d. all of the above are characteristics of managerial accounting

2. Henry Scherck is an stockbroker. In this capacity, Henry is interested in which of the following kinds of information?
   a. information that pertains to the operations of a business such as time cards and work schedules
   b. information that is global and pertains to the business as a whole
   c. information that pertains to the subunits of a business organization
   d. both a and c

3. Which of the following is **not** a product cost?
   a. The cost of ordering production supplies
   b. The cost of rent on the manufacturing facility
   c. The cost of commissions paid to sales staff.
   d. a and c

4. Which of the following statements concerning product versus general, selling, and administrative (GS&A) costs is true?
   a. Product costs are usually spread between the balance sheet and the income statement
   b. GS&A costs never appear on the balance sheet
   c. Product costs appear only on the income statement
   d. GS&A costs are accumulated in an inventory account before appearing on the income statement

The following information applies to the next two questions:

Nunamaker Industries (NI) makes baby diapers. During the most recent accounting period, NI paid $90,000 for raw materials, $78,000 for labour, and $82,000 for overhead costs that were incurred to make boxes. Brock started and completed 125,000 boxes. GS&A Expenses amounted to $120,000.

5. Assuming NI desires to earn a gross profit that is equal to 60% of product cost. The selling price should be:
   a. $2.00
   b. $2.60
   c. $3.00
   d. $3.20

6. If NI sells 110,000 boxes of diapers, the amount of net income will be:
   a. $12,000
   b. $13,200
   c. $22,000
   d. none of the above

7. Which of the following statement is true?
   a. A cost can be recognized as an expense immediately or accumulated in an asset account
   b. A cost and an expense are different terms used to describe the same thing
   c. An expense can be recognized immediately or accumulated in an asset account
   d. Costs incurred for wages of production workers are expensed before they are accumulated in an inventory account

The following information applies to the next two questions:

During 20X1, Galloway Manufacturing Company (GMC) incurred $280,000 of manufacturing costs and $84,000 of GS&A expenses. GMC made 14,000 units of product and sold 12,000 units.

8. Based on the above information, the balance in the inventory account shown on GMC's 12/31/X1 balance sheet is:
   a. $220,000
   b. $40,000
   c. $280,000
   d. $24,000

9. Based on the above information, the amount of expense shown on GMC's 12/31/X1 income statement is:
   a $240,000
   b. $84,000
   c. $324,000
   d. none of the above

10. Caster Company paid cash for the rental of manufacturing equipment. Select the answer that shows the effect that this event would have on the financial statements.

	Assets	= Liab.	+Equity	Rev.	− Exp.	= Net Inc.	Cash Flow
a.	−	n/a	−	n/a	−	−	n/a
b	− +	n/a	n/a	n/a	n/a	n/a	− OA
c.	−	n/a	−	n/a	n/a	n/a	− OA
d.	+ −	n/a	n/a	n/a	n/a	n/a	n/a

The following information applies to the next three questions:

The accounting records of the Ariyo Manufacturing Company (AMC) contained the following information:

Raw Materials Used	$40,000	Sales Revenue	$192,000
Sales Salaries	12,000	Indirect Manufacturing Costs	68,000
Amortization on Admin. Equip.	8,000	Amortization on Production Equip.	14,000
Wages Paid to Production Workers	60,000	Miscellaneous GS&A Expenses	18,000

AMC made 5,000 units of product and sold 4,000 units during the accounting period. There was no beginning inventory.

11. AMC average product cost per unit is:
    a. $33.60
    b. $16.40
    c. $20.00
    d. $36.40

12. The balance in AMC's inventory account as of December 31 is:
    a. $36,400
    b. $145,600
    c. $33,600
    d. $182,000

13. The amount of net income appearing on AMC's December 31 income statement is:
    a. $26,400
    b. $34,400
    c. $8,400
    d. $46,400

14. The president of Betts Manufacturing Company is paid an incentive bonus that is equal to 5% of net income. During the current accounting period, Betts expects to make 10,000 units of product and to sell 9,000 units. Betts recently incurred a $1,000,000 manufacturing design cost. There is a debate regarding whether this cost should be classified as a product cost or as an upstream cost. Betts is in a 30% tax bracket. Based on this information, select the true answer from the following choices:
    a. The company president will be motivated to classify the cost as a product cost because her bonus will be $50,000 higher than it will be if the cost is classified as an upstream cost.
    b. Betts income taxes expense will be $70,000 more if the design cost is classified as a product cost than it will be if it is classified as an upstream cost.
    c. Betts financial statements will portray a more favorable financial position if the design cost is classified as an upstream cost rather than a product cost.
    d. None of the statements is true.

15. The accountant for Shaw Manufacturing mistakenly classified a selling expense as a product cost during an accounting period in which the company sold more inventory than it produced. Shaw uses a LIFO cost flow system. As a result of this error,
    a. assets and net income will be overstated.
    b. assets will be overstated and net income will be understated.
    c. assets and net income will be understated.
    d. assets and net income will be unaffected.

16. Which of the following practices is not considered to be an emerging trend in managerial accounting?
    a. Benchmarking
    b. Value-added assessment
    c. Stereotyping
    d. Activity-based management

17. Which of the following cost is **not** incurred by service companies?
    a. raw materials cost
    b. labour cost
    c. overhead cost
    d. service companies incur all of the above costs.

Exercise Type Problems

P1. Leneau Manufacturing Company makes a high quality picture frame that is sold to photo shops. The company was started on January 1, 20X3 when it issued common shares in return for $140,000 in cash from shareholders. During 20X3 the company purchased and used raw materials that cost $36,400 cash. Wages paid to workers who made the frames amounted to $47,700 cash. Finally, Leneau paid $46,100 cash for manufacturing overhead costs. The company started and completed the production of 14,000 frames during 20X3. The sales price was established at cost plus $6. Leneau sold 12,000 frames for cash during 20X3. GS&A expenses amounted to $51,500 cash.

Required:

1. The problem description references seven distinct business events (the recognition of sales revenue and the recognition of cost of goods sold are considered separate events). Identify these seven events and the dollar amounts associated with each event.

2. Record the events in T-accounts.

3. Prepare an income statement, balance sheet, and cash flow statement.

P1. Form for Requirement 1

The seven events are:
1.
2.
3.
4.
5. Recognized sales of . . .

   Sales Price determined as follows:

   Materials
   Labour
   Overhead   _____
   Total Product Cost   +   units =   cost per frame

   Price = Cost Per Frame + $6.00 =

6.
7.

P1. Form for Requirement 2

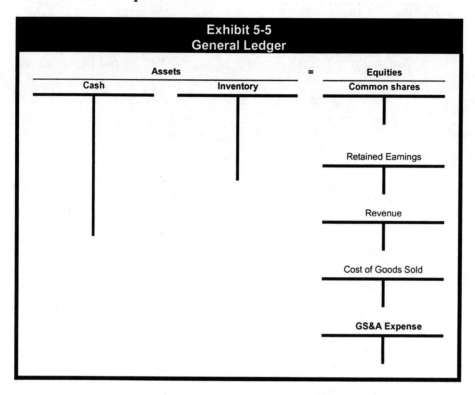

P1. Form for Requirement 3

Leneau Manufacturing Company Financial Statements December 31, 20X3	
INCOME STATEMENT	
Revenue	
Cost of Goods Sold	
Gross Margin	
GS&A Expenses	
Net Income	$ 20,500
BALANCE SHEET	
Assets	
Cash	
Inventory	
Total Assets	$160,500
Equity	
Common shares	
Retained Earnings	
Total Equity	
CASH FLOW STATEMENT	
Cash Flows from Operating Activities	
Cash Receipts from Revenue	
Cash Payments for Inventory	
Cash Payments for Expenses	
Net Cash Flows from Operating Activities	
Cash Flows from Investing Activities	
Cash Flows from Financing Activities	
Cash Receipts from Capital Acquisition	
Net Change in Cash	
Plus Beginning Cash Balance	
Ending Cash Balance	$141,900

P2. Mulholland Manufacturing Company was started on January 1, 20X3. The company engaged in following accounting events during its first year of operation. With the exception of the adjusting entries for amortization, assume that all transactions are cash transactions.

1. Issed common shares in return for $50,000 in cash from shareholders.
2. Paid $8,000 for the materials that were used to make its products. All products started were completed during the period.
3. Paid salaries of $3,200 to selling and administrative employees.
4. Paid wages of $9,500 to production workers.
5. Paid $6,800 for furniture used in selling and administrative offices.
6. Recognized amortization on the selling and administrative office furniture. The furniture was acquired on January 1. It had an $800 estimated salvage value and a 3 year useful life.
7. Paid $12,500 for manufacturing equipment.
8. Recognized amortization on the manufacturing equipment. The equipment was acquired on January 1. It had a $500 estimated salvage value and a 4 year useful life.
9. Sold inventory to customers for $30,000.
10. Recognized cost of goods sold amounting to $17,000.

Required: Explain how these events would affect the balance sheet, income statement, and cash flow statement by recording them in a horizontal financial statements model as indicated below. In the cash column, use the initials OA to designate operating activity, IA for investing activity, and FA for financing activity. The first event is recorded as an example.

P2. Form for Financial Statements Model

Event No.	Cash	+ Inventory	+ Manuf. Equip.*	+ Office Furn.*	= Com. Shares	+ Ret. Ear.	Rev.	− Exp.	= Net Inc.	Cash Flow
1	50,000 +	+	+	+	= 50,000	+		−	=	50,000 FA
2	+	+	+	+	=	+		−	=	
3	+	+	+	+	=	+		−	=	
4	+	+	+	+	=	+		−	=	
5	+	+	+	+	=	+		−	=	
6	+	+	+	+	=	+		−	=	
7	+	+	+	+	=	+		−	=	
8	+	+	+	+	=	+		−	=	
9	+	+	+	+	=	+		−	=	
10	+	+	+	+	=	+		−	=	
Totals	40,000 +	3,500 +	9,500 +	4,800	= 50,000 +	7,800	30,000	−22,200	= 7,800	40,000

* Record accumulated amortization as negative amounts under these columns.

P3. The following trial balance was drawn from the records of Schlafly Manufacturing Company (SMC) as of December 31, 20X2.

Account Titles	Debit	Credit
Cash	$60,000	
Common shares		$40,000
Retained Earnings		20,000
Totals	$60,000	$60,000

During the 20X3, the SMC incurred specifically identifiable product costs (i.e., materials, labour and overhead) amounting to $34,000. In addition, SMC incurred a $12,000 manufacturing design costs. SMC's accounting staff was in disagreement as to how this design cost should be classified. Some members of the staff thought that the cost should be classified as a product cost (i.e., option no. 1) others believed it should be considered a GSA expense (i.e., option no. 2). During 20X3 SMC made 5,000 units of product and sold 4,000 units at a price of $14 each. All transactions were cash transactions.

Required:

1. Prepare an income statement, balance sheet, and cash flow statement under each of the two options.

2. Identify the option that results in financial statements that are more likely to leave a favorable impression on investors and creditors.

3. Assume that SMC provides an incentive bonus to the company president that is equal to 10% of net income. Compute the amount of the bonus under each of the two options. Identify the option that provides the president with the higher bonus.

4. Assume a 30% income tax rate. Determine the amount of income tax expense under each of the two options. Identify the option that minimizes the amount of the company's income tax expense.

P3. Form for Requirement 1

Schlafly Manufacturing Company Financial Statements December 31, 20X3		
INCOME STATEMENT	**Option 1**	**Option 2**
Revenue		
Cost of Goods Sold		
Gross Margin		
GS&A Expenses		
Net Income	$19,200	$16,800
BALANCE SHEET		
Assets		
Cash		
Inventory		
Total Assets	$79,200	$76,800
Equity		
Common shares		
Retained Earnings		
Total Equity	$79,200	$76,800
CASH FLOW STATEMENT		
Cash Flows from Operating Activities		
Cash Receipts from Revenue		
Cash Payments for Inventory		
Cash Payments for Expenses		
Net Cash Flows from Operating Activities		
Cash Flows from Investing Activities		
Cash Flows from Financing Activities		
Net Change in Cash		
Plus Beginning Cash Balance		
Ending Cash Balance	$70,000	$70,000

P4. Bob Strobel sells helium balloons in Hill Park on Saturdays as a means of making some extra spending money. He buys balloons from a party store at a cost of $1.20 each and sells them at a price of $3.00 each. Demand for the balloons ranges between 35 and 45 per day. Bob normally purchases 40 balloons. The helium looses its resilience in a couple of days, so balloons not sold cannot be saved for the following Saturday. Bob usually just releases the balloons that do not sell. As he watched the most recent batch of five balloons floating into space, he thought surely, there must be some way to avoid this waste.

Required:

1. If Bob buys 40 balloons and sells 35, what is the amount of profit that he will earn? What is the cost of waste due to excess inventory?

2. If Bob buys 40 balloons and has the opportunity to sell 45, what is the amount of profit that he will earn? What is the amount of opportunity cost that will be incurred?

3. Bob has the opportunity to rent a helium canister that would enable him to fill balloons while working in the park. Renting the canister would cost $8 per day. Deflated balloons can be purchased at a price of $1.00 each. Should Bob rent the canister or continue to buy ready-filled balloons. What is the name of the type of inventory system Bob would be using if he supplies his customers balloons on demand?

P4. Form for Requirement 1

Revenue (35 x $3.00)	
Cost of Goods Sold (40 x $1.20)	
Net Income	

P4. Form for Requirement 2

Revenue (40 x $3.00)	
Cost of Goods Sold (40 x $1.20)	
Net Income	

Multiple Choice Problems - Solutions

1. d   Refer to Exhibit 1-2 in the text for a summary of the differences between managerial and financial accounting.

2. b   A stockbroker is more interested in comparing the financial performance of companies taken as a whole rather than the detailed operating reports of the subunits of an organization.

3. c   All costs incurred for the purpose of manufacturing products are classified as product costs. Since the supplies and rent are used in the manufacturing process, they are product costs. If the supplies had been used for administrative or selling purposes, the cost of ordering them would have been a GS&A expense.

4. a   GS&A cost may appear on the balance sheet (e.g., office equipment) and the income statement (e.g., amortization or salary expense), but will never appear in the inventory account. Product cost pass through an inventory account (i.e., balance sheet account) before appearing on the income statement as cost of goods sold.

5. d

Materials	$90,000		
Labour	78,000		
Overhead	82,000		
Total Product Cost	$250,000	+ 125,000 boxes	= $2.00 cost per box
Sales Price	$2.00 x 1.6	= $3.20 per box	

6. a

Sales (110,000 units x $3.20)	$ 352,000
Cost of Goods Sold (110,000 x $2.00)	(220,000)
Gross Margin	132,000
GS&A Expense	(120,000)
Net Income	$ 12,000

7. a

8. b

    $280,000 + 14,000 = $20 cost per unit of product.
    There are 2,000 units of product in ending inventory (i.e., 14,000 – 12,000)
    The balance in ending inventory is: 2,000 units x $20 per unit = $40,000.

9. c

Cost of goods sold (12,000 units x $20 per unit)	$240,000
GS&A Expenses	84,000
Total Expenses	$324,000

10. b   The event is an asset exchange. Cash would decrease and inventory increase. The income statement is not affected. The cash outflow is classified as an operating activity.

11. d

Materials	$40,000
Labour	60,000
Indirect Manufacturing Costs	68,000
Amortization on Production Equip.	14,000
Total Product Cost	$182,000 ÷ 5,000 units = $36.40 cost per unit

12. a

There are 1,000 units of product in ending inventory (i.e., 5,000 – 4,000)
The balance in ending inventory is: 1,000 units x $36.40 per unit = $36,400.

13. c

Sales	$ 192,000
Cost of Goods Sold (4,000 x $36.40)	(145,600)
Gross Margin	46,400
Sales Salaries	(12,000)
Amortization on Admin. Equip.	(8,000)
Miscellaneous GS&A Expense	(18,000)
Net Income	$ 8,400

14. d   If the design cost is classified as a product cost $100,000 (i.e., $1,000,000 / 10,000 units = $100 x 1,000 units = $100,000) of the cost will remain in the inventory account at the end of the accounting period. This means that assets and net income will be $100,000 higher if the cost is classified as a product costs rather than an upstream cost. Accordingly, the portrayal of financial position would be more positive, the manager's bonus would be $5,000 (i.e., $100,000 x .05) higher, and taxes would be $30,000 (i.e., $100,000 x .30) higher than they would be if the cost is classified as a product cost. This analysis ignores interrelationships between the variables. For example, the fact that the president's bonus would affect the amount of net income, which would affect the amount of taxes, is ignored.

15. d   If the number of units sold is greater than the number of units produced all costs placed into the inventory account during the period plus some of the costs in the beginning inventory balance will have been expensed as cost of goods sold. Accordingly, the misclassification will have passed through the accounts and total assets and net income will be correct by the end of the accounting period. Some selling expenses will be misclassified as cost of goods sold, but the total amount of expenses recognized will be correct.

16. c

17. d   Service companies, like manufacturing companies, incur materials, labour, and overhead costs in the process of providing services to their customers. The primary difference between manufacturing entities and service companies is that the products provided by service companies are consumed immediately. Accordingly, service companies normally do not have an inventory account.

Exercise Type Problems - Solutions

P1. Solution for Requirement 1

The seven events are:
1. Issued common shares in return for $14,000 in cash from shareholders.
2. Paid $36,400 cash for raw materials used to make frames.
3. Paid $47,700 for labour used to make frames.
4. Paid $46,100 for overhead costs incurred to make frames.
5. Recognized sales of $183,600 (12,000 frames at a price of $15.30).

    Price determined as follows:

Materials	$36,400
Labour	47,700
Overhead	46,100
Total Product Cost	$130,200

    $130,200 ÷ 14,000 units = $9.30 cost per frame

    Price = $9.30 + $6.00 = $15.30

6. Recognized $111,600 cost of goods sold (12,000 frames at a cost of $9.30 each).
7. Recognized GS&A expenses of $51,500

P1. Solution for Requirement 2

Exhibit 5-5
General Ledger

Assets = Equities

Cash				Inventory				Common shares	
(1) 140,000	36,400 (2)			(2) 36,400	111,600 (6)				140,000 (1)
(5) 183,600	47,700 (3)			(3) 47,700					
	46,100 (4)			(4) 46,100					
	51,500 (7)			Bal 18,600					
Bal 141,900									

Retained Earnings

	20,500 (cl.)
	20,500 Bal.

Sales Revenue

(cl.) 183,600	183,600 (5)
	-0- Bal.

Cost of Goods Sold

(7) 111,600	111,600 (cl.)
Bal. -0-	

GS&A Expense

(7) 51,500	51,500 (cl.)
Bal. -0-	

P1. Solution for Requirement 3

Leneau Manufacturing Company
Financial Statements
December 31, 20X3

INCOME STATEMENTS
Revenue	$183,600
Cost of Goods Sold	(111,600)
Gross Margin	72,000
GS&A Expenses	(51,500)
Net Income	$ 20,500

BALANCE SHEETS
Assets
Cash	$141,900
Inventory	18,600
Total Assets	$160,500

Equity
Common shares	$140,000
Retained Earnings	20,500
Total Equity	$160,500

CASH FLOW STATEMENT
Cash Flows from Operating Activities
Cash Receipts from Revenue	$183,600
Cash Payments for Inventory	(130,200)
Cash Payments for Expenses	(51,500)
Net Cash Flows from Operating Activities	$ 1,900
Cash Flows from Investing Activities	-0-
Cash Flows from Financing Activities	
Cash Receipts from Capital Acquisition	140,000
Net Change in Cash	$141,900
Plus Beginning Cash Balance	0
Ending Cash Balance	$141,900

P2. Solution

Event No.	Cash	+ Inventory	+ Manuf. Equip.*	+ Office Furn.*	= Com. Shares	+ Ret. Ear.	Rev.	− Exp.	= Net Inc.	Cash Flow
1	50,000 +	+	+	+	= 50,000	+	−	=	50,000 FA
2	(8,000) +	8,000 +	+	+	=	+	−	=	(8,000) OA
3	(3,200) +	+	+	+	=	+ (3,200)	−	3,200 =	(3,200)	(3,200) OA
4	(9,500) +	9,500 +	+	+	=	+	−	=	(9,500) OA
5	(6,800) +	+	+	+ 6,800	=	+	−	=	(6,800) IA
6	+	+	+ (2,000)	=	+ (2,000)	−	2,000 =	(2,000)	
7	(12,500) +	+ 12,500	+	+	=	+	−	=	(12,500) IA
8	+	3,000 +	(3,000) +	+	=	+	−	=	
9	30,000 +	+	+	+	=	+ 30,000	30,000 −	=	30,000	30,000 OA
10	+	(17,000) +	+	+	=	+ (17,000)	−	17,000 =	(17,000)	
Totals	40,000 +	3,500 +	9,500 +	4,800	= 50,000 +	7,800	30,000 −	22,200 =	7,800	40,000

* Record accumulated amortization as negative amounts under these columns.

P3. Solution for Requirement 1

Schlafly Manufacturing Company Financial Statements December 31, 20X3		
INCOME STATEMENT	**Option 1**	**Option 2**
Revenue	$56,000	$56,000
Cost of Goods Sold	36,800[1]	27,200[2]
Gross Margin	$19,200	$28,800
GS&A Expenses		(12,000)
Net Income	$19,200	$16,800
[1] ($34,000 + $12,000)/ 5,000 = $9.20 x 4,000 = $36,800		
[2] $34,000 / 5,000 = $6.80 x 4,000 = $27,200		
BALANCE SHEET		
Assets		
Cash	$70,000[3]	$70,000[3]
Inventory	9,200	6,800
Total Assets	$79,200	$76,800
[3] $60,000 − $34,000 − $12,000 + $56,000 = $70,000		
Equity		
Common shares	$40,000	$40,000
Retained Earnings	39,200	36,800
Total Equity	$79,200	$76,800
CASH FLOW STATEMENT		
Cash Flows from Operating Activities		
Cash Receipts from Revenue	$56,000	$56,000
Cash Payments for Inventory	(46,000)	(34,000)
Cash Payments for Expenses		(12,000)
Net Cash Flows from Operating Activities	10,000	10,000
Cash Flows from Investing Activities	-0-	-0-
Cash Flows from Financing Activities	-0-	-0-
Net Change in Cash	10,000	10,000
Plus Beginning Cash Balance	60,000	60,000
Ending Cash Balance	$70,000	$70,000

P3. Solution for Requirement 2

Option 1 produces statements with higher amounts of assets and net income. It is therefore more likely to leave a favorable impression on investors and creditors.

P3. Solution for Requirement 3

Option 1: $19,200 x .10 = $1,920; **Option 2:** $16,800 x .10 = 1,680; Option 1 produces the higher bonus.

P3. Solution for Requirement 4

Option 1: $19,200 x .30 = $5,760; **Option 2:** $16,800 x .30 = $5,040; Option 2 minimizes taxes.

P4. Solution for Requirement 1

Revenue (35 x $3.00)	$105
Cost of Goods Sold (40 x $1.20)	(48)
Net Income	$ 57

Five Balloons would have been wasted (i.e., 40 – 35). At a cost of $1.20 each, the amount waste is $6 (i.e., 5 x $1.20).

P4. Solution for Requirement 2

Revenue (40 x $3.00)	$120
Cost of Goods Sold (40 x $1.20)	(48)
Net Income	$ 72

Bob lost the opportunity to sell five additional balloons. Bob earns a contribution margin of $1.80 (i.e., $3.00 – $1.20) per balloon. The amount of the opportunity loss is $9.00 (i.e., 5 x $1.80).

P4. Solution for Requirement 3

Bob should rent the canister. The cost of 40 inflated balloons is $48 (i.e., $1.20 x 40). The cost of 40 deflated balloons plus the canister is $48 (i.e., $1.00 x 40 = $40 + $8 = $48). Accordingly, the cost of 40 balloons is the same regardless of whether the canister is rented. However, the canister would enable Bob to produce balloons as they are needed, thereby eliminating waste or opportunity cost. The inventory system that permits you to provide inventory as customers demand it is called *just-in-time inventory*.

Chapter 2
Cost Behaviour, Operating Leverage, and Profitability Analysis

Learning Objectives for the Chapter

The material in this chapter of the study guide is designed to facilitate your ability to:

- Distinguish between fixed and variable cost behaviour..
- Understand how operating leverage affects profitability.
- Understand how cost behaviour affects profitability.
- Prepare an income statement under a contribution margin approach.
- Calculate the magnitude of operating leverage.
- Use cost behaviour to create a competitive operating advantage.
- Understand how cost behaviour is affected by the relevant range and the decision making context.
- Select an appropriate time period for the calculation of the average cost per unit.
- Define the term mixed-cost.
- Use the high/low method, scattergraphs, and regression to estimate fixed and variable costs.

Brief Explanation of the Learning Objectives

Distinguish between fixed and variable cost behaviour.

The following table shows the behaviour pattern of a fixed cost. Specifically, the table shows the amount of total cost and cost per unit for compensation paid to a teacher who has 15, 20, or 25 students in a workshop.

Units of Product Sold (a)	15	20	25
Total Expected Compensation Cost (b)	$7,500	$7,500	$7,500
Average **Per Unit** [i.e., per student] Cost (b ÷ a)	$500	$375	$300

As the terminology implies, total fixed cost is fixed (i.e., stays the same) when the volume of activity (i.e., number of students) changes. In contrast, the fixed cost per unit varies (i.e., changes) when the level of activity changes. This results in a *logical inconsistency in terminology*. Specifically, *fixed cost per unit exhibits a variable behaviour pattern*. *Be careful*, the failure to recognize this inconsistency will diminish your ability to identify cost behaviour.

The following table shows the behaviour pattern of a **variable cost**. Specifically, the table shows the amount of total cost and cost per unit of books that cost $30 each provided to 15, 20, or 25 students in a workshop.

Units of Product Sold (a)	15	20	25
Total Expected Compensation Cost (b)	$450	$600	$750
Average **Per Unit** [i.e., per student] (b ÷ a)	$30	$30	$30

As the terminology implies, total variable cost varies (i.e., changes) with changes in the volume of activity (i.e., number of students). In contrast, the variable cost per unit is fixed (i.e., stays the same) regardless of the level of activity. This results in a *logical inconsistency in terminology*. Specifically, *variable cost per unit exhibits a fixed behaviour pattern*. Here also, the failure to recognize this inconsistency will diminish your ability to identify cost behaviour.

Understand how operating leverage affects profitability.

The practice of using a fixed cost structure to leverage a small percentage change in revenue into a large percentage change in profitability is called **operating leverage**. *When costs are fixed, percentage increases and decreases in revenue have a disproportionate impact on profitability.* To illustrate, assume a starting point of $5 of revenue and $3 of fixed costs resulting in $2 of profit. If revenue increases by $1, profits will increase by $1 because costs are fixed and not affected by the change in revenue. The $1 increase in revenue represents a 20% (i.e., $1 / $5 = .20) increase while the $1 increase in profitability represents a 50% (i.e., $1 / $2 = .50) increase. Accordingly, a 20% increase in revenue results in a 50% increase in profitability.

When costs are variable, percentage increases and decreases in revenue have a proportionate impact on profitability. To illustrate, assume a starting point of $5 of revenue and $3 of variable costs resulting in $2 of profit. If revenue increases by 20% costs will increase by 20%, thereby resulting in a proportionate (i.e., 20%) increase in profitability. As proof, revenue will be $6 (i.e., $5 x 1.2); variable cost will be $3.60 (i.e., $3 x 1.2) resulting in a profit of $2.40 (i.e., $6.00 − $3.60). The $0.40 (i.e., $2.40 − $2.00) increase in profitability represents a 20% increase (i.e., $0.40 / $2.00). Accordingly, a 20% increase in revenue results in a 20% increase in profitability. In other words, there is no operating leverage when costs are purely variable.

Since the changes in profitability are leveraged when costs are fixed, a fixed cost structure offers a greater opportunity to improve profitability. Unfortunately, this effect holds on the downside as well as the upside. This means a small decrease in revenue will produce a large decrease in profitability. Accordingly, a fixed cost structure holds a greater risk of incurring a loss. As a example, suppose you decide to sponsor a concert an offer to pay the band $20,000 regardless of the number of ticket sales (i.e., the cost of the band is fixed). If no tickets are sold, you lose $20,000. On the other hand, you could contract to pay the band $5 per ticket sold (i.e., a variable cost). In this case if no tickets are sold, you lose nothing. In general, a fixed cost structure offers greater risks and rewards than does a variable cost structure.

Prepare an income statement under a contribution margin approach.

To prepare an income statement under the contribution margin approach, variable costs are subtracted from revenue to determine the amount of contribution margin. Fixed costs are subtracted from the contribution margin to determine the amount of net income. An example is shown below.

Sales Revenue	$220
Variable Cost	(60)
Contribution margin	$160
Fixed Cost	(120)
Net Income	$40

Calculate the magnitude of operating leverage.

The magnitude of operating leverage can be calculated by dividing the contribution margin by the net income. Using the data in the contribution margin income statement shown above, the magnitude of operating leverage is:

Contribution margin / Net Income = $160 / $40 = 4 times

The result suggests that the percentage change in profitability will be four times any percentage change in revenue. In other words, if revenue increase by 20%, profitability will increase by 80% (i.e., 20% x 4).

Understand how cost behaviour is affected by the relevant range and the decision making context.

Costs behaviour (i.e., fixed or variable) holds over some designated range of activity known as the **relevant range**. For example, the cost of renting a room in which a workshop is conducted is fixed within a range of 1 to 25 people. If more than 25 people attend the workshop, it will be necessary to rent another room, which would increase the rental cost. If zero people attend the workshop, the room will not be rented and the cost will decrease. Only within the relevant range (1 to 25 people) will the cost remain fixed.

The exact same cost can be classified as fixed under one set of circumstances and variable under a different set of circumstances. To illustrate, assume that an instructor is paid $7,500 per workshop regardless of the number of students attending the workshop. While the cost of instruction is fixed relative to the number of students attending a single workshop, it is a variable cost relative to the number of workshops conducted.

Select an appropriate time period for the calculation of the average cost per unit.

Accountants focus on average costs because they are relatively easy to compute and are frequently more relevant to decision making than actual costs. Computing the average cost per unit requires considering the span of time from which data are drawn. For example, you could determine the average cost that was incurred during a day, a week, a month, a year, etc. In general, shorter time periods contain data that is more current than data drawn from longer periods. The average cost incurred yesterday is more current information than the average cost incurred last year. Unfortunately, shorter time periods include less data points, which can lead to greater distortion. Yesterday may have been an odd day that is not representative of what is likely to happen tomorrow. Selecting the most appropriate time period requires judgment.

Define the term mixed-cost.

A mixed cost is a cost that is partially fixed and partially variable. For example, the cost of a telephone normally includes a monthly charge that is fixed regardless on the number of local calls made plus an additional charge that varies in relation to the number of minutes the phone is used for long-distance calls.

Use the high/low method, scattergraphs, and regression to estimate fixed and variable costs.

The high/low method is a mathematical procedure that can be used to estimate the variable cost per unit and the total amount of fixed. The procedure begins with the identification of the highest and lowest level of activity in a data set that shows total costs at different levels of activity. Once the high and low activity points have been selected, the variable cost per unit can be determined as follows:

$$\frac{\text{Variable Cost}}{\text{Per Unit}} = \frac{\text{Cost at High Point} - \text{Cost at Low Point}}{\text{Volume at High Point} - \text{Volume at Low Point}}$$

Once the variable cost per unit has been determined the, fixed cost component can be determined by subtracting the variable cost from the total cost at either the high point or the low point. The formulas for the appropriate computations are as follow:

Fixed Cost + (Variable Cost Per Unit x No. of Units) = Total Cost
Fixed Cost = Total Cost − (Variable Cost Per Unit x No. of Units)

Self-Study Problems

Multiple Choice Problems

1. When volume increases:
   a. fixed cost in total increases and fixed cost per unit decreases.
   b. fixed cost in total remains constant and fixed cost per unit decreases.
   c. fixed cost in total and fixed cost per unit remain constant.
   d. none of the above.

2. When volume increases:
   a. variable cost in total increases and variable cost per unit decreases.
   b. variable cost in total remains constant and variable cost per unit decreases.
   c. variable cost in total and variable cost per unit increase.
   d. none of the above.

3. At a point when volume reached 4,000 units, fixed costs amounted to $20,000 and total cost amounted to $60,000. If volume were to increase to a level of 5,000 units, total cost would be:
   a. $70,000
   b. $60,000
   c. $100,000
   d. none of the above

4. The following income statement was produced when the volume of sales was 200 units.

Sales Revenue	$1,000
Variable Cost	(600)
Contribution margin	$400
Fixed Cost	(150)
Net Income	$250

   If volume reaches 250 units, net income will be:
   a. $350
   b. $500
   c. $550
   d. none of the above

5. Complete the following table assuming the cost is a **fixed** cost.

Units of Product Sold	15	20	25
Total Expected Cost	$7,500		"X"
Average **Per Unit**	$500		"Y"

The amounts in the cells labeled "X" and "Y" is, respectively

a. $12,500 and $500
b. $7,500 and $500
c. $12,500 and $625
d. $7,500 and $300

6. Complete the following table assuming the cost is a **variable** cost.

Units of Product Sold	15	20	25
Total Expected Cost	$7,500		"X"
Average **Per Unit**	$500		"Y"

The amounts in the cells labeled "X" and "Y" is, respectively

a. $7,500 and $500
b. $12,500 and $625
c. $12,500 and $500
d. $7,500 and $300

The Following Information Pertains to the Next Four Questions:
Joe's Bait and Tackle Company operates a chain of convenience stores that are located on lakes throughout the United States. The company pays rent of $12,000 a year for each store. Inventory is purchased as needed. The managers of each shop are paid a salary of $1,200 a month and all other employees are paid on an hourly basis.

7. Relative to the number of volume of sales, the *cost of rent* at each store is what kind of cost?
   a. variable cost
   b. mixed cost
   c. historical cost
   d. fixed cost

8. Relative to the number of stores, the ***cost of rent*** is which kind of cost?
   a. fixed cost
   b. variable cost
   c. mixed cost
   d. accumulated cost

9. The ***costs of inventory*** relative to the volume of sales in a particular shop and relative to the volume of sales in the entire chain of stores is which kind of cost, respectively?
   a. variable cost / fixed cost
   b. fixed cost / fixed cost
   c. variable cost / variable cost
   d. variable cost / fixed cost

10. Relative to the number of hours worked, total employee compensation cost for a particular store and for a chain of stores is which kind of cost, respectively?
    a. variable cost / variable cost
    b. fixed cost / fixed cost
    c. mixed cost / mixed cost
    d. fixed cost / variable cost

11. Within the relevant range, the total cost remains constant when volume increases. However, when volume exceeds the relevant range, the total cost increases. The type of cost behaviour is called
    a. variable cost behaviour.
    b. mixed cost behaviour.
    c. fixed cost behaviour.
    d. allocated cost behaviour.

12. Operating leverage is possible when the organizational cost structure is:
    a. purely fixed.
    b. purely variable.
    c. mixed.
    d. a or c.

13. Zegna Company sells men's sports coats. The average sales price is $475 the average cost per coat is $225. Fixed costs are $4,220,000. If Zegna sells 25,000 coats, the contribution margin will be:
    a. $7,655,000.
    b. $5,625,000.
    c. $2,030,000.
    d. $6,250,000.

14. Ritts Company sells waste containers. The price and cost of the containers is $75 and $40, respectively. Fixed costs are $210,000. Ritts sells approximate 8,000 containers per year. Based on this information, the magnitude of operating leverage is:
    a. 3 times.
    b. 4 times.
    c. 5 times.
    d. 6 times.

15. Blanchett Stapler Company sells staplers at a price of $7 each. The staplers cost $4 each. Blanchett sold 10,000 staplers during its most recent accounting period. Fixed costs amounted to $20,000. If the number of units sold increases by 10%, profitability will increase by which of the following amounts?
    a. 10%
    b. 20%
    c. 30%
    d. 40%

16. Jasper Motor Sports sells and services jet skis. To operate the services department, the fixed cost per week is expected to be $1,700. Variable costs are expected to be $25 per ski?

    Number of skis serviced during the last week was :

Mon	Tues	Wed	Thrs	Fri	Sat	Sun
16	10	20	12	40	50	22

    The weekly average cost to service each jet ski is:
    a. $25
    b. $35
    c. $40
    d. None of the above

The following information applies to the next two questions.
Herrera Company operates manufacturing facilities. The following data represent the volume of production and total cost of production for each facility.

Facility	Units	Total Cost
1	700,000	$400,000
2	500,000	$280,000
3	200,000	$120,000
4	680,000	$420,000
5	210,000	$118,000

17. The variable cost per unit is which of the following?
    a. $2.80
    b. $0.50
    c. $0.28
    d. $0.56

18. The total fixed cost is which of the following?
    a. $8,000
    b. $280,000
    c. $500,000
    d. $5,600

Exercise Type Problems

P1. Martha Hurley rents a car that she drives to and from school. The car rental agreement stipulates that daily kilometers are unlimited. Martha is responsible for gas. She also pays an $8 fee per day for insurance.

Required ■

Classify each of the following costs incurred by Martha as being fixed, variable or mixed.
1. The insurance cost relative to the number of days the car is rented.
2. The insurance cost relative to the number of kilometers the car is driven on a particular day.
3. The gasoline cost relative to the number of kilometers driven.
4. The gasoline cost relative to the number of days the car is rented and driven.
5. The total cost of renting and operating the car relative to the number of kilometers driven in one day for one day.

P2. Kiell Publishing Company produces and sells an outdoor sports magazine. The company has fixed cost of $533,120. The variable cost averages $1.50 per magazine. During 20X5 Kiell produced and sold 392,000 copies of the magazine at a price of $3.50 each.

Required:
1. Prepare an income statement using the contribution margin format.

2. Assume Kiell experiences a 20% growth rate in the number of magazines sold, prepare a revised income statement and determine the amount of the percentage growth rate in profitability.

3. What has caused the percentage growth rate in profitability to be larger than the percentage growth rate in revenue?

4. If the number of units sold were to decline by 20% instead of grow by that amount, would net income decline by 20% or more than 20%? Explain you answer.

P2. Form for Requirement 1

Sales Revenue	
Variable Cost	
Contribution margin	
Fixed Cost	
Net Income	$ 250,880

P2. Form for Requirement 2

Sales Revenue	
Variable Cost	
Contribution margin	
Fixed Cost	
Net Income	$ 407,680

P3. The following income statement was prepared by the accountant of Friend Company.

Sales Revenue ($12 x 8,000 units)	$96,000
Variable Cost ($8 x 8,000 units)	(64,000)
Contribution margin	32,000
Fixed Cost	-0-
Net Income	$32,000

Required:

1. If Friend experiences a 14% increase in the number of units sold, speculate as to the size of the resulting percentage increase in net income?

2. Validate you answer to *requirement 1* by preparing a revised income statement and determining the amount of the percentage change in profitability.

P3. Form for Requirement 2

Sales Revenue	
Variable Cost	
Contribution margin	
Fixed Cost	
Net Income	

P4. Peretz Company makes and sells rugs. The average sales price is $1,280. The average cost per rug is $690. Fixed costs amounts to $354,000. The company sells 800 rugs.

Required:

1. Determine the magnitude of operating leverage?

2. Use the answer computed in requirement 1 to estimate the percentage change in profitability that would occur in sales increase by 9%.

P4. Form for Requirement 1

(Hint: Begin by preparing an income statement under a contribution margin format)

Sales Revenue	
Variable Cost	
Contribution margin	
Fixed Cost	
Net Income	$118,000

P5. Czelandnicki Company owns six retail stores. The following data represent the dollar volume of sales and total cost of operating for each store.

Store	Sales in $	Total Cost
1	920,000	$612,000
2	500,000	$380,000
3	400,000	$330,000
4	580,000	$370,000
5	320,000	$252,000
6	340,000	$250,000

Required:

1. Use the high/low method to estimate the variable cost per dollar of sales?

2. Estimate amount of fixed cost (base your estimate on the low point in the data set).

P5. Form for Requirement 1

$$\frac{\text{Variable Cost}}{\text{Per Unit}} = \frac{\text{Cost at High Point} - \text{Cost at Low Point}}{\text{Volume at High Point} - \text{Volume at Low Point}}$$

$$\frac{\text{Variable Cost}}{\text{Per Unit}} = \underline{\hspace{5in}}$$

Multiple Choice Problems - Solutions

1. b

2. d   When volume increases variable cost in total increases and variable cost per unit remains constant.

3. a   At 4,000 Units
Total Cost = Fixed Cost + Variable Cost
Variable Cost = Total Cost − Fixed cost
Variable Cost = $60,000 − $20,000
Variable Cost = $40,000
Variable Cost Per Unit = $40,000 / 4,000 = $10

At 5,000 Units
Total Cost = Fixed Cost + Variable Cost
Total Cost = $20,000 + ($10 x 5,000) = $70,000

4. a   At 200 Units
Sales Price = $1,000 / 200 = $5
Variable Cost Per Unit = $600 / $200 = $3

Sales Revenue ($5 x 250 units)	$1,250
Variable Cost ($3 x 250 units)	(750)
Contribution margin	$500
Fixed Cost	(150)
Net Income	$350

5. d   Total Fixed Cost remains constant at $7,500
Fixed cost per unit = $7,500 / 25 = $300

6. c   Total Variable Cost = $500 cost per unit x 25 units = $12,500
Variable Cost Per Unit remains constant

7. d   Within the relevant range, the cost of rent for a particular store will remain constant no matter what volume of sales.

8. b   The more stores rented the higher the total rent cost.

9. c   When sales volume increases, the total cost of inventory will increase for each store and for the entire chain of store.

10. c   When the number of hours worked increases, the salary of the store manager remains constant but the total cost wages paid to other workers increases. This is true whether one store or the entire chain of stores is considered.

11. c   Cost is classified based on how it behaves within the relevant range. Behaviour outside the relevant range is irrelevant. Within the relevant range, a cost that remains constant when volume increases is called a fixed cost.

12. a There are 1,000 units of product in ending inventory (i.e., 5,000 – 4,000)
The balance in ending inventory is: 1,000 units x $36.40 per unit = $36,400.

13. d The contribution margin is equal to the amount of sales revenue minus variable cost. In this case;

Sales Revenue ($475 x 25,000 units)	$11,875,000
Variable Cost ($225 x 25,000 units)	(5,625,000)
Contribution margin	$ 6,250,000

14. b The magnitude of operating leverage is computed by dividing the contribution margin by the amount of net income. Begin by preparing an income statement under the contribution margin approach as follows:

Sales Revenue ($75 x 8,000 units)	$600,000
Variable Cost ($40 x 8,000 units)	(320,000)
Contribution margin	280,000
Fixed Cost	(210,000)
Net Income	$70,000

Magnitude of Operating Leverage = $280,000 / $70,000 = 4 times

15. c The answer can be determined in two ways. The quickest way is to determine the magnitude of operating leverage and multiplying it times the percentage increase in revenue. Begin by preparing an income statement in a contribution margin format.

Sales Revenue ($7 x 10,000 units)	$70,000
Variable Cost ($4 x 10,000 units)	(40,000)
Contribution margin	30,000
Fixed Cost	(20,000)
Net Income	$10,000

Magnitude of Operating Leverage = $30,000 / $10,000 = 3 times
% Change in Profitability = % Change in Revenue x Magnitude of Operating Leverage
10% x 3 = 30%

The problem can also be solved by re-computing the amount of net income assuming a 10% growth in sales (i.e., 10,000 units x 1.1 = 11,000 units. The income statement would appear as follows:

Sales Revenue ($7 x 11,000 units)	$77,000
Variable Cost ($4 x 11,000 units)	(44,000)
Contribution margin	33,000
Fixed Cost	(20,000)
Net Income	$13,000

The percentage change in net income is ($13,000 – $10,000) / $10,000 = 30%

16. b The total number of skis serviced during the week is: 16+10++20+12+40+50+22=170.
The total weekly cost is: $1,700 fixed + (170 x $25) variable = $5,950
The average cost per jet ski is: $5,950 / 170 = $35

17. d

$$\frac{\text{Variable Cost}}{\text{Per Unit}} = \frac{\text{Cost at High Point} - \text{Cost at Low Point}}{\text{Volume at High Point} - \text{Volume at Low Point}}$$

$$\frac{\text{Variable Cost}}{\text{Per Unit}} = \frac{400{,}000 - 120{,}000}{700{,}000 - 200{,}000}$$

Variable Cost Per Unit = $280,000 / 500,000 = $0.56

18. a At the high point:
Fixed Cost + (Variable Cost Per Unit x No. of Units) = Total Cost
Fixed Cost = $400,000 − ($0.056 x 700,000)
Fixed Cost = $8,000

Exercise Type Problems - Solutions

P1. Solution for Requirements 1-5
1. Variable – Since insurance costs are charged each day, total insurance costs will increase as the number of days rented increases.
2. Fixed – The total daily insurance cost stays the same regardless of the number of kilometers the car is driven.
3. Variable – Gasoline costs will increase as the number of kilometers driven increases.
4. Variable – Gasoline costs will increase the more the car is rented and driven.
5. Mixed – Rental and insurance cost will remain fixed regardless of the number of kilometers driven. However, gasoline costs will vary in proportion to the number of kilometers driven. Accordingly, total cost contains a fixed and a variable component.

P2. Solution for Requirement 1

Sales Revenue ($3.50 x 392,000 units)	$1,372,000
Variable Cost ($1.5 x 392,000 units)	(588,000)
Contribution margin	784,000
Fixed Cost	(533,120)
Net Income	$ 250,880

P2. Solution for Requirement 2
The number of units sold assuming a 20% growth rate is 470,400 (i.e., 392,000 x 1.2). An income statement assuming 470,400 are sold is shown below.

Sales Revenue ($3.50 x 470,400 units)	$1,646,400
Variable Cost ($1.5 x 470,400 units)	(705,600)
Contribution margin	940,800
Fixed Cost	(533,120)
Net Income	$ 407,680

The percentage in profitability is 62.5% [i.e., ($407,680 – 250,880) / 250,880].

P2. Solution for Requirement 3

The condition wherein a fixed or mixed cost structure is used to leverage growth rates of revenue into higher growth rates of profitability is called operating leverage.

P2. Solution for Requirement 4

If revenue declines by 20% profitability will decline by more than 20%. Since the company has fixed costs, it will experience some degree of operating leverage. As a result of operating leverage, any given percentage change in revenue will produce a magnified percentage change in profitability. The phenomenon occurs regardless of whether the percentage change in revenue is an increase or a decrease.

P3. Solution for Requirement 1

Since Friend Company has no fixed cost, there will be no operating leverage effect. When all costs are variable, any percentage change in revenue will bring a proportionate change in net earnings. Therefore, as a result of the 14% increase in sales, you can expect a proportionate 14% increase in net income.

P3. Solution for Requirement 2

A 14% increase would result in sales of 9,120 (8,000 x 1.14)

Sales in Units (a)	8,000	9,120
Sales Revenue ($12 x a)	$96,000	$109,440
Variable Cost ($8 x 8,000 units)	(64,000)	(72,960)
Contribution margin	32,000	36,480
Fixed Cost	-0-	-0-
Net Income	$32,000	$ 36,480

The change in net income is, in fact, 14% [i.e., (36,480 – 32,000) / 32,000].

P4. Solution for Requirement 1

Begin by preparing an income statement under a contribution margin format.

Sales Revenue ($1,280 x 800)	$1,024,000
Variable Cost ($690 x 800 units)	(552,000)
Contribution margin	472,000
Fixed Cost	(354,000)
Net Income	$ 118,000

Magnitude of Operating Leverage = Contribution margin / Net Income
Magnitude of Operating Leverage = $472,000 / 118,000 = 4 times

P4. Solution for Requirement 2

The magnitude of operating leverage computed in requirement 1 suggests that net income will increase by 4 times the amount of the percentage increase in revenue. Accordingly the expected percentage increase in net income is 36% (i.e., 9% x 4).

P5. Solution for Requirement 1

$$\frac{\text{Variable Cost}}{\text{Per Unit}} = \frac{\text{Cost at High Point} - \text{Cost at Low Point}}{\text{Volume at High Point} - \text{Volume at Low Point}}$$

$$\frac{\text{Variable Cost}}{\text{Per Unit}} = \frac{612{,}000 - 252{,}000}{920{,}000 - 320{,}000}$$

Variable Cost Per Unit = $360,000 / 600,000 = $0.60 per sales dollar

P5. Solution for Requirement 2

Fixed Cost + (Variable Cost Per Sales Dollar x No. of Sales Dollars) = Total Cost
Fixed Cost = $252,000 − ($0.060 x 320,000)
Fixed Cost = $60,000

Chapter 3
Analyzing Cost, Volume, and Pricing to Increase Profitability

Learning Objectives for the Chapter

The material in this chapter of the study guide is designed to facilitate your ability to:

- Determine the sales price of a product using a cost plus pricing approach.
- Use the contribution per unit approach to calculate the break-even point.
- Use the contribution per unit approach to calculate the sales volume required to attain a target profit.
- Use the contribution per unit approach to assess the effects of changes in sales price, variable costs, and fixed costs.
- Understand the concept of target pricing.
- Consider the ethical considerations associated with misleading advertising.
- Draw and interpret a cost-volume-profit graph.
- Calculate the margin of safety in units, dollars, and percentages.
- Understand how spreadsheet software can be used to conduct sensitivity analysis for cost-volume-profit relationships.
- Conduct cost-volume-profit analysis using the contribution margin ratio and the equation method.
- Identify the limitations associated with cost-volume-profit analysis.
- Perform multiple-product break-even analysis.

Brief Explanation of the Learning Objectives

Determine the sales price of a product using a cost plus pricing approach.

Cost plus pricing as used in this text is an approach to setting the sales price. The sales price is determined by calculating the cost of a product or service and adding a margin (usually expressed as a percentage of cost). For example, an item that cost $250 priced at cost plus a markup of 20% of cost would be priced at $300 [i.e., $250 + (250 x .20)].

The computation can be made in a variety of different ways. A common alternative is shown below:

(Cost x 1) + (Cost x .020) = Cost x 1.20 = 250 x 1.20 = $300

Using this approach for cost plus a 70% markup would be priced at $510 (i.e., $300 x 1.7) and cost plus a 110% markup would be priced at $630 (i.e., $300 x 2.1).

Use the contribution per unit approach to calculate the break-even point.

The per unit contribution margin is the difference between the sales price and the variable cost of a product or service. For example a product with a sales price and a variable cost of $75 and $50, respectively, would have a contribution margin of $25 (i.e., $75 − $50). This means that for every unit of this product sold, there will be $25 available to pay for fixed costs. Given $50,000 of fixed cost, it would require sales of 2,000 (i.e., $50,000 / $25) units of the product to be able to pay all of the fixed costs. The general formula for determining the break-even point is:

Fixed Costs / Contribution Margin Per Unit = Unit Sales Required to Break-even (i.e., earn a zero profit).

Use the contribution per unit approach to calculate the sales volume required to attain a target profit.

The number of units sold that is required to attain a desired profit can be computed by adding the profit component to the break-even formula. The result is as follows:

(Fixed Costs + Desired Profit) / Contribution Margin Per Unit = Unit Sales Required to a Desired Profit

To illustrate, assume a product with a sales price and a variable cost of $75 and $50, Fixed costs are $50,000 and the company desires to earn of profit of $20,000. The number of units of product that must be sold to attain this goal is:

Unit Sales Required to Earn a Desired Profit = (Fixed Costs + Desired Profit) / Contribution Margin Per Unit
Unit Sales Required to Earn a Desired Profit = ($50,000 + $20,000) / ($75 − $50)
Unit Sales Required to Earn a Desired Profit = 70,000 / $25
Unit Sales Required to Earn a Desired Profit = 2,800 units

Understand the concept of target pricing.

Target pricing is the inverse of the cost plus pricing approach. As shown above cost plus pricing starts with the determination of cost and from there develops the sales price. In contrast, target pricing starts with the determination of the sales price and works back to the cost that can be incurred to attain a desired profit objective. Research analysts, engineers and others in the production process seek to develop a product that can be made at a cost that will enable the company to meet its profit objectives and satisfy the consumer's pricing demands. To illustrate, assume a company has done market research that indicates consumers would be willing to pay $150 for an ultra-light cellular telephone. Further, assume that the company desires to earn a profit equal to $20 of cost. The target cost (i.e., the minimum cost at which the product can be made) is:

Sales Price Per Unit = (Target Cost Per Unit x 1.2)
Target Cost Per Unit = Sales Price Per Unit / 1.2
Target Cost Per Unit = $150 / 1.2
Target Cost Per Unit = $125

Draw and interpret a cost-volume-profit (CVP) graph.

The four steps required to prepare a CVP graph are summarized on page 92 of the textbook.

Calculate the margin of safety in units, dollars, and percentages.

The margin of safety is the difference between projected (budgeted) sales and break-even sales. It can be expressed in absolute amounts or in percentages. In addition, the margin of safety can be measured in units or in sales dollars. To illustrate, assume a company must sell 15,000 units of a product in order to break-even. Further, the company has budgeted sales of 18,000 units. The sales price is $12 per unit. The margin of safety is computed as follows:

In Absolute Amounts

	In Units (a)	In Dollars (a x $12)
Budgeted Sales	18,000	$216,000
Break-even Sales	(15,000)	(180,000)
Margin of Safety	3,000	$ 36,000

As a percentage

(Budgeted Sales – Break-even Sales) / Budgeted Sales
* Sales can be measured in either units or dollars, the computation using units is as follows:
(18,000 – 15,000) / 18,000 = 16.7%

Understand how spreadsheet software can be used to conduct sensitivity analysis for cost-volume-profit relationships.

The practice of assessing the sensitivity of profits to simultaneous changes in fixed costs, variable costs, and sales volume is know as **sensitivity analysis**. Spreadsheet software such as Excel can be used to rapidly assess the effects of a variety of different scenarios. The process begins by developing mathematical formulas that calculate profitability under an assortment of assumptions regarding costs and levels of activity. The formulas contain cell addresses where numbers representing the amount of costs and the levels of activity are located. When the numbers in the referenced cells change, the spreadsheet software automatically recalculates the amount of profitability. As a result, management can instantly retrieve answers to questions such as *what* happens to profitability *if* some combination of fixed costs, variable costs and volume change simultaneously. The computational power of the computer makes the variety of *what if* questions and instantaneous answers is virtually limitless.

Conduct cost-volume-profit analysis using the contribution margin ratio and the equation method.

Cost-volume-profit (CVP) relationships can be analyzed using a variety of mathematical formulas. Three possibilities are discussed in this chapter. Two of these are the per unit contribution margin approach and the contribution margin ratio approach. Recall that the contribution ratio is calculated by dividing the per unit contribution margin by the sales price. The formulas for determining the sales volume required to attain a desired level of profitability under the two contribution margin approaches are as follows.

Per Unit Contribution Approach Sales Volume in Units	Contribution Ratio Approach Sales Volume in Dollars
$\dfrac{\text{Fixed Costs + Desired Profit}}{\text{Contribution Margin Per Unit}}$ = Units	$\dfrac{\text{Fixed Costs + Desired Profit}}{\text{Contribution Margin Ratio}}$ = Dollars

The third method of analyzing CVP relationships is called the equation method. The formula for determining the sales volume required to attain a desired level of profitability under the equation method is:

(Sales Price x No. of Units) = (Variable Cost Per Unit x No. of Units) + Fixed Cost + Desired Profit

Identify the limitations associated with cost-volume-profit analysis.

The accuracy of cost-volume-profit analysis is limited due to the fact that it assumes a strictly linear relationship among the variables. However, the linearity among actual CVP variables is the exception rather than the norm. Secondly, CVP assumes that such factors as worker efficiency are constant over the range of the activity analyzed. Frequently businesses are able to increase productivity but CVP formulas are not constructed to allow for such changes in efficiency.

Self-Study Problems

Multiple Choice Problems

1. Ruettgers Company makes Caller ID boxes. In the process of making 15,000 boxes Ruettgers incurred the following costs: Materials $120,000; Labour $105,000; and overhead $150,000. Ruettgers prices its products at cost plus 40%. Based on this information the price per box charged by Ruettgers is:
   a. $25
   b. $35
   c. $40
   d. none of the above

2. Tse Manufacturing Company uses target costing. Tse's marketing team has determined that customers would be willing to pay $20 each for an electric pencil sharpener. Tse plans to make and sell 10,000 sharpeners and desires to earn a gross profit that is equal to 25% of cost of goods sold. Based on this information, the total target cost for the 10,000 sharpeners is
   a. $160,000
   b. $250,000
   c. $150,000
   d. none of the above

3. The following information was drawn from the records of Clark Company

Sales Price	$9 per unit
Variable Cost	$6 per unit
Fixed Cost	$24,000
Units Sold	8,600

   Based on this information the break-even point is:
   a. sales of 8,600 units
   b. sales of $32,600
   c. sales of 8,000 units
   d. sales of $24,000

4. Trace Sales Corporation sold 5,000 units of a product at a price of $4 each. Total variable cost amounted to $10,000 and fixed costs amounted to $8,000. Based on this information, the break-even point is:
   a. sales of 3,000 units
   b. sales amounting to $18,000
   c. sales amounting to $20,000
   d. sales of 4,000 units

5. Strickland reached it breakeven point when sales reached 4,000 units. Fixed cost amounted to $60,000 and variable cost per unit was $3. Based on this information the sales price per unit is:
   a. $18
   b. $12
   c. $15
   d. none of the above

6. Shah Enterprises (SE) desires to earn a profit of $81,984. SE has total fixed cost of $240,000. The company sells a product that cost $42 each for a price of $74 each. Based on this information, the level of required sales necessary to attain the company's profit objective is:
   a. 10,000 units
   b. 2,562 units
   c. 10,062 units
   d. 2,500 units

7. Canant Company makes glass figurines that are sold for $200 each. During an accounting period in which 6,000 figurines were made and sold, production costs amounted to $900,000 of which $660,000 were variable. General, selling and administrative cost were $200,000 of which $120,000 were variable. Based on this information the contribution margin per unit is:
   a. $110.00
   b. $130.00
   c. $183.33
   d. none of the above

The following information applies to the next two questions.

Doster, Inc. makes and sells 65,000 units of a product that has a contribution margin of $14 per unit. Variable costs are $8 per unit and fixed costs amount to $728,000. Dosser has an opportunity to purchase new production equipment. The equipment will increase fixed cost by $124,000 and reduce variable cost by $2 per unit. The sales volume will remains at 65,000 units and the sales price will not change if the new production equipment is purchased.

8. Without giving consideration to the possible purchase of the new production equipment, the sales price per unit of Doster's product is:
   a. $6
   b. $22
   c. $28
   d. none of the above

9. If Doster purchases the new production equipment...
   a. profitability will decrease by $6,000.
   b. profitability will decrease by $14,000.
   c. Profitability will increase by $6,000.
   d. Profitability will increase by $14,000.

Use the following graph to answer the next two questions:

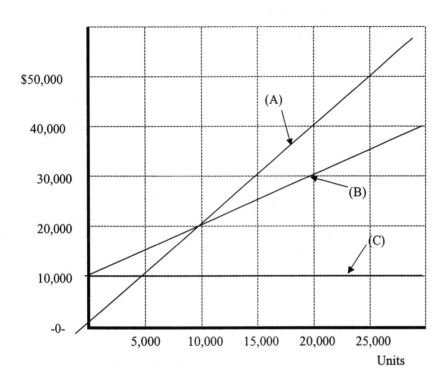

11. Based on the above graph, break-even point, total revenue is?
    a. Zero
    b. $10,000
    c. $20,000
    d. $30,000

12. Based on the above graph, select the true answer.
    a. The line represented by the letter (B) is the revenue line.
    b. The sales price is $2.00 per unit.
    c. The line represented by the letter (A) shows how total cost would behave relative to the units being produced.
    d. At the break-even point, fixed cost is equal to $20,000.

This information pertains to the next two problems

Laubach Legal Services Company (LLSC) has fixed costs of $96,000 and variable costs of $120 per hour of service rendered. Clients are charged an hourly rate of $220 per hour. According to LLSC's budget, the company expects to provide clients with 1,200 hours of service.

13. LLSC's margin of safety expressed as a percentage of budgeted hours is:
    a. 80%
    b. 40%
    c. 20%
    d. 10%

14. LLSC's margin of safety expressed in sales dollars is:
    a. $52,800
    b. $264,000
    c. $211,200
    d. none of the above

15. Two companies have the exact same sales price, fixed cost and variable cost. The break-even point for both companies is 1,200 units. Company A is currently selling 1,400 units and Company B is selling 1,500 units of product. Based on this information:
    a. Company A has a greater magnitude of operating leverage than Company B.
    b. Company B has a greater magnitude of operating leverage than Company A.
    c. Company A and Company B have the same magnitude of operating leverage.
    d. The answer cannot be determined from the information provided.

Exercise Type Problems

P1. Lake Smith Company (LSC) makes and sells boat docks. The variable cost of each dock is $12,000. Docks are sold for $20,000 each. Fixed costs amount to $240,000.

Required:
1. Calculate the break-even point expressed in units using the per unit contribution margin approach.

2. Calculate the break-even point expressed in sales dollars using the contribution margin ratio.

3. Calculate the break-even point expressed in units and sales dollars using the equation method.

4. Determine the sales volume in units and dollars that would be required to attain a profit of $160,000. Verify your answer by preparing an income statement using the contribution margin format.

5. Determine the margin of safety between sales required to attain the desired profit (i.e., here after called desired sales) and the break-even sales volume. Express the margin of safety as a percentage.

6. Prepare a break-even graph using the cost and price assumptions outlined above.

P1. Form for Requirement 1

Break-even in Units = Fixed Cost / Contribution Margin Per Unit

P1. Form for Requirement 2

Contribution Margin Ratio = Contribution Margin Per Unit / Sales Price Per Unit

Break-even in Dollars = Fixed Cost / Contribution Margin Ratio

P1. Form for Requirement 3

Sales Price x Units = Fixed Cost + Variable Cost x Units

Sales Dollars = Sales Price x Units

P1. Form for Requirement 4

Sales Volume in Units = Fixed Cost + Desired Profit / Contribution Margin Per Unit

P1. Form for Requirement 5

Margin of Safety = (Desired Sales – Break-even Sales) / Desired Sales

P1. Form for Requirement 6

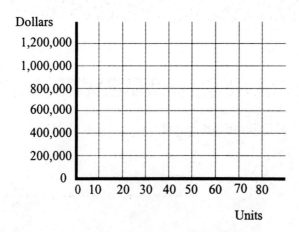

P2. Sekorsky and Company makes and sells 42,000 units of a product at an average price of $47 per unit. Variable costs are $27 per unit and fixed costs amount to $620,000. Consider each of the following requirements as being independent of the other requirements.

Required:
1. The marketing department believes that it could sell 10,000 additional units (52,000 in total) if the sales price were lowered to $39 per unit. Should Sekorsky lower the price? Support you answer with appropriate computations.

2. Sekorsky has the opportunity to purchase new equipment that will enable the Company to lower labour costs thereby reducing the variable cost per unit to $22. The purchase of the equipment will act to raise fixed cost by $60,000 (total fixed cost will become $680,000. Should Sekorsky purchase the equipment? Support you answer with appropriate computations.

3. Sekorsky is considering an opportunity to improve the quality of its product. To accomplish the improvement, the company would have to increase fixed costs by $100,000 bringing the total to $720,000. Further, variable cost will increase by $5 per unit bringing the total variable cost per unit to $32. The product improvement is expected to increase the number of units sold by 8,000 units bringing total sales to 50,000 units. Further, the sales price will increased to $50. Should Sekorsky undertake the project to improve the quality of its product? Support you answer with appropriate computations.

P2. Form for Requirement 1

	Before Price Change	After Price Change
Sales Price Per Unit (a)		
Sales Volume in Units (b)		
Variable Cost Per Unit (c)		
Income Statements		
Sales Revenue (a x b)		
Variable Cost (b x c)		
Contribution Margin		
Fixed Cost		
Net Income		

P2. Form for Requirement 2

	Before Purchase	After Purchase
Sales Price Per Unit (a)		
Sales Volume in Units (b)		
Variable Cost Per Unit (c)		
Income Statements		
Sales Revenue (a x b)		
Variable Cost (b x c)		
Contribution Margin		
Fixed Cost		
Net Income		

P2. Form for Requirement 3

	Before Quality Improvement	After Quality Improvement
Sales Price (a)		
Sales Volume (b)		
Variable Cost Per Unit (c)		
Income Statements		
Sales Revenue (a x b)		
Variable Cost (b x c)		
Contribution Margin		
Fixed Cost		
Net Income		

Solutions for Multiple Choice Problems

1. b   Cost Per Unit = ($120,000 + $105,000 + $150,000) / 15,000 = $25
   Sales Price = Cost + (Cost x .40) = $25 x 1.4 = $35

2. a   Target Cost Per Unit + (Target Cost Per Unit x .25) = $20
   1.25 x Target Cost Per Unit = $20
   Target Cost Per Unit = $20 / 1.25 = $16
   Total Target Cost for 10,000 sharpeners = $16 x 10,000 = $160,000

3. c   Break-even = Fixed Cost / Contribution Margin Per Unit = $24,000 / ($9 – $6) = 8,000 Units

4. d   Variable Cost Per Unit = $10,000 / 5,000 = $2
   Contribution Margin Per Unit = Sales Price Per Unit – Variable Cost Per Unit = $4 – $2 = $2
   Break-even = Fixed Cost / Contribution Margin Per Unit = $8,000 / $2 = 4,000 Units

5. a   Sales Price x No. of Units = Fixed Cost + (Variable Cost Per Unit x No. of Units)
   Sales Price x 4,000 = $60,000 + ($3 x 4,000)
   Sales Price x 4,000 = $72,000
   Sales Price = $72,000 / 4,000 Units = $18

6. c   Sales Required to Earn Desired Profit = (Fixed Cost + Desired Profit) / Contribution Margin Per Unit
   Sales Required to Earn Desired Profit = ($240,000 + $81,984) / ($74 – $42) = 10,062 units

7. d   Variable Cost Per Unit = Total Variable Cost / Units = ($660,000 + $120,00) / 6,000 = $130
   Contribution Margin Per Unit = Sales Price Per Unit – Variable Cost Per Unit = $200 – $130 = $70

8. b   Sales Price = Variable Cost + Contribution Margin = $8 + $14 = $22

9. c

	Before Purchase	After Purchase
Sales Price (a)	$22	$22
Sales Volume (b)	65,000 Units	65,000 Units
Variable Cost Per Unit (c)	$8	$6
Income Statements		
Sales Revenue (a x b)	$1,430,000	$1,430,000
Variable Cost (b x c)	(520,000)	(390,000)
Contribution Margin	910,000	1,040,000
Fixed Cost	(728,000)	(852,000)
Net Income	$ 182,000	$ 188,000

Difference = Net Income After Purchase – Net Income Before Purchase
Difference = $188,000 – $182,000 = $6,000 Increase

11. c.

12 b. $20,000 / 10,000 units = $2.00 per unit

Further Explanation
The line represented by the letter (B) is the total cost line.
The line represented by the letter (A) is the total revenue line.
Fixed cost is $10,000 at any volume of activity

13 c.   Break-even in Units = Fixed Cost / Contribution Margin = $96,000 / ($220 – $120) = 960 Hours
Margin of Safety as a % = (Budgeted Sales – Break-even Sales) / Budgeted Sales
Margin of Safety as a % = (1,200 Hours – 960 Hours) / 1,200 Hours = 20%

14 a.   Margin of Safety in Sales Dollars = Budgeted Sales in Dollars – Break-even Sales in Dollar) /
Margin of Safety in Sales Dollars = (1,200 Hours x $220) – (960 hours x $220) = $52,800

15 a.   The magnitude of operating leverage is determined by the following formula: (Contribution Margin / Net Income). As volume increases, the contribution margin grows steadily. As you approach the break-even point the amount of net loss/ income will decrease and increase there after. Accordingly, the magnitude of operating leverage will increase as a company approaches the break-even point and decrease thereafter. Since Company A is closer to the break-even point than is Company B, Company A will have greater magnitude operating leverage.

Solutions to Exercise Type Problems

P1. Solution for Requirement 1

Break-even in Units = Fixed Cost / Contribution Margin Per Unit
Break-even in Units = $240,000 / ($20,000 – $12,000) = 30 Units

P1. Solution for Requirement 2

Contribution Margin Ratio = Contribution Margin Per Unit / Sales Price Per Unit
Contribution Margin Ratio = ($20,000 – $12,000) / $20,000 = .40
Break-even in Dollars = Fixed Cost / Contribution Margin Ratio
Break-even in Dollars = $240,000 / .40 = $600,000

P1. Solution for Requirement 3

Sales Price x Units = Fixed Cost + Variable Cost x Units
($20,000 x Units) = $240,000 + ($12,000 x Units)
($20,000 – $12,000) x Units = $240,000
Units = $240,000 / $8,000 = 30 Units

Sales Dollars = Sales Price x Units
Sales Dollars = $20,000 x 30 = $600,000

P1. Solution for Requirement 4

Sales Volume in Units = Fixed Cost + Desired Profit / Contribution Margin Per Unit
Sales Volume in Units = $240,000 + $160,000 / ($20,000 – $12,000) = 50 Units
Sales Volume in Dollars = Sales Price x Units = $20,000 x 50 = $1,000,000

P1. Solution for Requirement 5

Margin of Safety = (Desired Sales − Break-even Sales) / Desired Sales
Margin of Safety = ($1,000,000 − $600,000) / 1,000,000 = 40%

P1. Form for Requirement 6

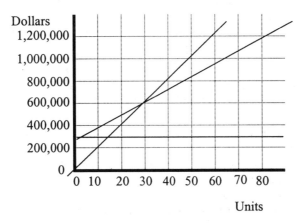

P2. Solution for Requirement 1

	Before Price Chang	After Price Chang
Sales Price (a)	$47	$39
Sales Volume (b)	42,000 Units	52,000 Units
Variable Cost Per Unit (c)	$27	$27
Income Statements		
Sales Revenue (a x b)	$1,974,000	$2,028,000
Variable Cost (b x c)	(1,134,000)	(1,404,000)
Contribution Margin	840,000	624,000
Fixed Cost	(620,000)	(620,000)
Net Income	$ 220,000	$ 4,000

The statements suggest that it would be unwise for Sekorsky to lower the sales price.

P2. Solution for Requirement 2

	Before Purchase	After Purchase
Sales Price (a)	$47	$47
Sales Volume (b)	42,000 Units	42,000 Units
Variable Cost Per Unit (c)	$27	$22
Income Statements		
Sales Revenue (a x b)	$1,974,000	$1,974,000
Variable Cost (b x c)	(1,134,000)	(924,000)
Contribution Margin	840,000	1,050,000
Fixed Cost	(620,000)	(680,000)
Net Income	$ 220,000	$ 370,000

The statements suggest that it would be wise for Sekorsky to purchase the equipment.

P2. Solution for Requirement 3

	Before Quality Improvement	After Quality Improvement
Sales Price (a)	$47	$50
Sales Volume (b)	42,000 Units	50,000 Units
Variable Cost Per Unit (c)	$27	$32
Income Statements		
Sales Revenue (a x b)	$1,974,000	$2,500,000
Variable Cost (b x c)	(1,134,000)	(1,600,000)
Contribution Margin	840,000	900,000
Fixed Cost	(620,000)	(720,000)
Net Income	$ 220,000	$ 180,000

The statements suggest that it would be unwise for Sekorsky to undertake the project to improve the quality of its product.

Chapter 4
Relevant Information for Special Decisions

Learning Objectives for the Chapter

The material in this chapter of the study guide is designed to facilitate your ability to:

- Identify the characteristics of relevant information.
- Recognize sunk costs and understand why these costs are not relevant in decision making.
- Understand what the term *differential* revenue means.
- Understand what the terms *avoidable* and *differential* cost mean.
- Distinguish between unit-level, batch-level, product-level, and facility-level costs and understand how these costs are involved in decision making.
- Understand that relevance is a unique concept and its application is context sensitive.
- Identify opportunity costs and understand why these costs are relevant in decision making.
- Distinguish between quantitative vs. qualitative characteristics of decision making.
- Perform analysis leading to appropriate decisions for special order, outsourcing, segment elimination, and asset replacement decisions.
- Understand the conflict between short and long run profitability.
- Perform the analysis necessary to make decisions regarding the allocation of scarce resources.

Brief Explanation of the Learning Objectives

Identify the characteristics of relevant information.

To be relevant, information must (1) be future oriented and (2) differ between the alternatives.

Recognize sunk costs and understand why these costs are not relevant in decision making.

A sunk cost is a cost that has been incurred in the past. Since the cost was incurred in the past, it represents a historical fact that applies equally to (is the same for) all alternatives associated with a current decision. Since a sunk cost does not differ between the alternatives, it is not relevant. To illustrate, suppose Smith Company previously paid $80,000 for land that now has a market value of $70,000. Suppose further that Smith now must decide whether to use the land as a building site or to sell it for $70,000.

Selling the land at a loss or using it for a plant site will not change the fact that the company originally paid $80,000 for it. The $80,000 has already been incurred regardless of which alternative is selected. Since the original cost of the land is the same regardless of whether it is used for a plant site or is sold, it is not relevant to making a choice between the alternatives.

Understand what the term *differential* revenue means.

As the name implies differential revenues are revenues that differ between decision alternatives. For example, if a special order is accepted revenue will be different than it will be if the special order is rejected.

Understand what the terms *avoidable* and *differential* cost mean.

Differential costs are costs that differ between decision alternatives. If a cost differs between two alternatives, it can be avoided by selecting the alternative that does not include the cost. More specifically, if Alternative A requires an expense that is not required by Alternative B, that expense can be avoided by selecting Alternative B. Accordingly, differential costs are sometimes called avoidable costs. For example, the cost of renting a manufacturing facility can be avoided if the manufacturing operation is eliminated. Similarly, if Alternative A requires a $3,000 operating expense while Alternative B requires a $2,000 operating expense, $1,000 of the differential operating expense can be avoided by selecting Alternative B.

Distinguish between unit-level, batch-level, product-level, and facility-level costs and understand how these costs are involved in decision making.

Costs can be classified into one of four categories including:

a. **Unit-level costs** increase or decrease each time a unit of product is added or subtracted from the production process. Examples include direct labour and direct materials.

b. **Batch-level costs** increase or decrease each time a batch is added or subtracted from the production process. Examples include setup cost and quality testing.

c. **Product-level costs** increase or decrease each time a product or product-line is added or subtracted from the production process. An example is legal costs that increase each time a publishing company files for a copyright for a new book. Likewise, engineering costs increase each time an automobile company adds a new model to its product line. The distinguishing feature here is between new products versus more units of the same product.

d. **Facility-level costs** increase or decrease each time a new facility is added or an existing facility is eliminated. Examples include factory amortization, maintenance, utilities, etc.

These classifications are useful in identifying revenues and costs that are relevant to different types of special decisions. The relationships between the type of decision and the cost categories are described below.

a. **Special order decisions** involve an offer to sell additional units of an existing product. *When confronted with a special order problem, complete the following steps. (1) determine the relevant cost of making and selling the additional units of the product. (2) determine the additional revenue that will be generated by selling the additional units of product. (3) accept the special order if the additional revenues calculated in step 2 exceed the relevant cost calculated in step 1.* Relevant costs associated with making and selling additional units of a product include the unit-level costs and possibly the batch-level costs. If the additional units can be added to an existing batch, the batch-level costs represent sunk costs that have already been incurred and are therefore not relevant. If a new batch must be started to make the additional units, then the additional batch-level costs are relevant because they could be avoided if the special offer is rejected.

b. **Outsourcing decisions** involve choices between making a product and buying it from an outside third party. Accordingly, outsourcing decisions are frequently called "make or buy" decisions. *When confronted with an outsourcing problem complete the following steps. (1) determine the relevant cost of making the product. (2) determine the relevant cost of outsourcing (buying) the product. (3) compare the costs computed in steps 1 and 2 and select the lower cost.* Unit, batch, and product-level costs are relevant to outsourcing decisions. In general, these costs could be avoided if products were outsourced instead of being made internally. Note that some product-level cost may not be relevant to an outsourcing decision. For example, sales commissions for a product would continue regardless of whether the product was manufactured internally or purchased from a third party before being sold. Since facility-level costs will remain the same regardless of whether a product is outsourced, they are not avoidable and therefore are not relevant.

c. **Segment elimination decisions** involve choices between closing down or continuing to operate a segment of a business. *When confronted with a segement elimination decision complete the following steps. (1) determine the relevant cost of operating the segment. (2) determine the amount of revenue that is generated by the segment. (3) eliminate the segment if the revenue calculated in step 2 is less than the relevant cost calculated in step 1.* Unit, batch, product, and facility-level costs are relevant to a segment elimination decision. Note that some facility-level costs may not be relevant. For example, corporate-level facility costs (amortization of corporate headquarters, company president's salary, etc.) will continue even if a segment of the company is eliminated. Since these facility-level costs could not be avoided by eliminating the segment, they are not relevant to a decision regarding whether the segment should be eliminated.

Understand that relevance is a unique concept and its application is context sensitive.

The same exact cost can be fixed and relevant, variable and relevant, fixed and irrelevant or variable and irrelevant. In other words, cost behavior and relevance are independent concepts. Indeed, cost classification depends on the circumstances surrounding the decision at hand. To illustrate, consider the example of the salary of a store manager of a JCPenny store. The salary is a variable cost relative to the number of stores operated and is relevant to a decision regarding the elimination a store. The same salary cost is a fixed cost relative to the store's sales volume and is not relevant to a decision regarding the elimination of one of the departments that are operated in the store. The classification of cost into any of the categories depends on the circumstances associated with the decision-making environment. Change the circumstance and the cost classification will change. Accordingly, you must seek to understand the circumstances rather than memorize the definitions.

Identify opportunity costs and understand why these costs are relevant in decision making.

Many opportunities are mutually exclusive. In other words, reaping the benefits of one opportunity prohibits you from obtaining the benefits of an alternative opportunity. For example, if Smith Company (see illustration above related to sunk cost) uses the land for a building site, the Company loses the opportunity to obtain the $70,000 that could be acquired if the land were sold. Accordingly, using the land as a building site has a $70,000 opportunity cost. This is the relevant cost that must be considered in a decision regarding whether the land should be used for a building site or sold. As previously stated, the $80,000 original cost of the land is a sunk cost and is not relevant to a choice between selling the land and using it for a building site.

Distinguish between quantitative vs. qualitative characteristics of decision making.

Quantitative information, as used in this chapter, refers to the differential dollar values between one decision alternative and another decision alternative. Qualitative characteristics refer to the decision variables that cannot be measured in dollar values. For example, the cost of buying a part (outsourcing) may be cheaper than the cost of making it (quantitative information). However, outsourcing requires that you relinquish control over production schedules and quality (qualitative factors).

Be aware that this study guide focuses on the main ideas in the main body of text material. As such, it does not cover materials contained in the appendix.

Self-Study Problems

Multiple Choice Problems

1. Relevant information is:
   a. based on historical cost
   b. the same for all decision alternatives
   c. based on sunk cost
   d. none of the above

2. Tang Manufacturing Company is considering an opportunity to outsource a four function calculator that the Company currently makes and sales. Even if the calculator is outsourced, Tang plans to continue to sell it. Also, Tang plans to continue production on other calculator models that are currently being made by the Company. The costs associated with making the four function calculators include unit-level materials, labour, and overhead. In addition, there is some facility-level overhead costs that are allocated to the product. Tang pays a 5% sales commission on each calculator sold. Based on this information, indicate which of the following statements is false?
   a. The materials cost is relevant to the outsourcing decision.
   b. The facility-level overhead cost is not relevant to the outsourcing decision.
   c. The sales commission is relevant to the outsourcing decision.
   d. It may be wise for Tang to continue to manufacture the four function calculator even if the relevant cost of buying it is less than the relevant cost of making it.

3. Select the true statement.
   a. Fixed costs are never relevant.
   b. Variable costs are always relevant.
   c. A cost can be relevant or irrelevant depending on the circumstances.
   d. If you know whether a cost is fixed or variable, you will automatically know whether it is relevant or not.

4. Select the true statement.
   a. Unit-level costs are always relevant to special order decisions.
   b. Batch-level costs are never relevant to special order decisions.
   c. Product-level costs are always relevant to special order decisions.
   d. Statements *a* and *b* are ture.

5. Keck Enterprises, Inc. makes boat docks. A standard dock includes unit-level materials, labour, and overhead cost. In addition, the company incurs product-level engineering and advertising costs. The sales staff is paid a 10% commission on each dock sold. A sales person has located a land developer who is willing to purchase 12 docks only if he can buy them at an amount that is below Keck's current sales price. Which of the following costs would **not** be relevant to this special order decision?
   a. The unit-level materials, labour, and overhead costs
   b. The sales commissions
   c. The product-level engineering and advertising costs
   d. a and b

6. Dunkin Enterprises (DE) makes surge protectors that are used to protect equipment in electrical storms. The costs associated with making a surge protector are shown below.

   Unit-Level
   Materials $ 7.00
   Labour $12.00
   Overhead $ 3.00
   Batch-Level
   Set-up $4,000 per batch
   Product-Level
   Engineering $50,000 per year
   Advertising $120,000 per year

   Dunkin normally makes and sells 10,000 surge protectors per year which are made in batches containing 1,000 units. Dunkin has an opportunity to sell 1,000 protectors at a special order price of $24 per unit. Ignoring qualitative factors, Dunkin should

   a. accept the offer because it would increase profitability by $2,000
   b. reject the offer because it would decrease profitability by $2,000
   c. accept the offer because it would increase revenue by $240,000
   d. reject the offer because it would decrease profitability $4,000

The following information is available for the next **three (3)** questions:

   A production cost summary for Davidson Company follows:
   Unit-level direct material $5.00/unit
   Unit-level direct labour   2.00/unit
   Unit-level overhead   6.00/unit
   Product-level overhead   4.00/unit
   Total cost per unit $17.00

Fixed facility-level selling costs are $600,000 per year and unit-level selling costs are $2. The unit-level selling costs consist primarily of shipping and packaging costs. Production capacity is 400,000 units, but Davidson only expects to produce (and sell) 250,000 units next year. The normal selling price of the product is $30 per unit. A merchant from Venice, Italy has made an offer to purchase 50,000 units at $24 each.

7. The relevant incremental cost per unit associated with the special order is:
   a. $15
   b. $13
   c. $9
   d. $11

8. If Davidson accepts the special offer, profitability will:
   a. increase by $450,000
   b. decrease by $450,000
   c. increase by $550,000
   d. decrease by $550,000

9. Select the true statement from the following choices.
   a. The facility-level selling costs are relevant to the special offer decision.
   b. The product-level production costs are relevant to the special offer decision.
   c. The unit-level selling costs are not relevant to the special offer decision.
   d. All of the statements are false.

The following information is available for the next three (3) questions:
ROSS Industries manufactures a component with the following costs:

Unit-level material	$ 45
Unit-level labour	90
Unit-level overhead	30
Facility-level overhead	60
Total cost per unit	$225

ROSS uses 600 of the components each year. Agent Suppliers has offered to sell the component to ROSS for $202.50 each. Some members of management felt they could reduce costs by buying from Agent. If the component was purchased, ROSS could lease unused production facilities to a non-competing manufacturer for $9,000 per year.

10. What is the relevant cost of making the component?
    a. $135
    b. $165
    c. $180
    d. $224

11. If ROSS decides to purchase the 600 components that it currently makes, net income will
    a. increase by $13,500
    b. decrease by $13,500
    c. increase by $17,500
    d. decrease by $17,500

12. ROSS Company should...
    a. continue to manufacture the component.
    b. purchase the components to obtain a savings of $13,500.
    c. purchase the components if Agent reduces the price to $190.
    d. purchase the components at the offered price of $202.49.

13. Which of the following is a sunk cost?
    a. direct material
    b. direct labour
    c. wages of research & development people
    d. existing equipment

14. Rothco operates two segments. Income statements for both segments are shown below:

Segments	T	U
Sales	$500,000	$750,000
Unit -Level Variable Cost	(400,000)	(550,000)
Contribution Margin	100,000	200,000
Facility-Level Fixed Cost	(135,000)	(120,000)
Income (Loss)	(35,000)	80,000

    Management is considering discontinuing the operation of segment T. There would be no effect on total facility-level fixed costs, or sales and expenses of product U. By how much will company-wide income change, if segment T is eliminated?
    a. $35,000 decrease
    b. $35,000 increase
    c. $100,000 decrease
    d. $135,000 decrease

15. ABC Company is considering the replacement of a piece of manufacturing equipment. The old equipment originally cost $120,000. This equipment has a book value of $60,000 and a market value of $29,000. It has a remaining useful life of 4 years and a zero salvage value. Operating expenses for the old equipment are expected to be $9,000 per year. The new equipment has a purchase price of $54,000. It is expected to have a useful life of 4 years and a salvage value of $4,000. Operating expenses for the new equipment are expected to be $5,000 a year. If the old machine is replaced profitability will:
    a. increase by $5,000 over the next four years
    b. decrease by $5,000 over the next four years
    c. increase by $9,000 over the next four years
    d. decrease by $9,000 over the next four years

Exercise Type Problems

P1. Deal Dispenser Company (DDC) manufactures transparent tape dispensers. DDC has the capacity to produce 5,000,000 dispensers a year, but is currently producing and selling only 4,000,000 units a year. The normal selling price of a tape dispenser is $9. The unit-level costs associated with the production of a dispenser include: $2 for direct materials, $1.50 for direct labour, and $2.50 for indirect manufacturing costs. The total product- and facility-level costs to be incurred by DDC during the year are expected to be $2,300,000 and $1,200,000, respectively. Assume DDC receives a special order to produce and sell 200,000 dispensers at price of $7 each.

Required:
1. Calculate the relevant cost of making and selling an additional 200,000 dispensers.

2. Calculate the additional revenue associated with selling the 200,000 dispensers.

3. Make a recommendation regarding whether the special order should be accepted or rejected.

4. Comment on potential qualitative considerations.

P1. Form for Requirement 1

Unit-Level		
Materials		
Labour		
Overhead		
Total		$1,200,000

P1. Form for Requirement 2

P1. Form for Requirement 3

P1. Form for Requirement 4

P2. Safetyware, Inc. (SI) makes and sells life jackets. SI currently has an opportunity to purchase a comparable jacket from a reliable manufacturer at a price of $32 per jacket. SI currently makes 6,000 jackets per year. The costs associated with making the jackets are shown below.

Costs Associated with Making and Selling Life Jackets	
Cost of Materials (6,000 Units x $7)	$42,000
Labour (6,000 Units x $8)	48,000
Amortization on Manufacturing Equipment[1]	4,000
Salary of Production Supervisor	30,000
Product-Level Legal Costs	24,000
Rental Cost of Equipment Used to Make Jackets	12,000
Sales Commissions (6,000 Units x $8)	48,000
Fixed Selling Costs	29,000
Allocated Portion of Corporate Level Facility-Level Costs	15,000
Total Cost to Make 6,000 Jackets	$252,000

[1] The equipment has a book value of $28,000 but its market value is zero.

Required:
1. Determine the relevant cost of making the 6,000 jackets.

2. Determine the relevant cost of purchasing the 6,000 jackets.

3. Make a recommendation as to whether the jackets should be made or outsourced.

4. Comment on the relevance of the selling costs to this outsourcing decision.

P2. Form for Requirement 1

Relevant Costs Associated with Making Life Jackets	
Total Relevant Cost to Make 6,000 Jackets	$156,000

P2. Form for Requirement 2

P2. Form for Requirement 3

P2. Form for Requirement 4

P3. Harrold's Clothing Store operates a men's and women's department. The latest monthly income statement for each department and the company as a whole is shown below.

Segment	Men's	Women's	Total
Sales	$107,000	$224,000	$331,000
Cost of Goods Sold	(74,000)	(86,000)	(160,000)
Sales Commissions	(12,000)	(22,000)	(34,000)
Contribution Margin	21,000	116,000	137,000
Store Rent and General Fixed Overhead Cost	(28,000)	(42,000)	(70,000)
Store Manager's Salary	(10,000)	(10,000)	(20,000)
Department Manager's Salary	(6,000)	(8,000)	(14,000)
Advertising Expense	(5,000)	(10,000)	(15,000)
Net Income	$ (28,000)	$ 46,000	$ 18,000

Harold's recently received an offer to sublease the space in the store that is currently being used by the men's department at a rate of $11,000 per month.

Required:
1. Determine the relevant cost of operating the men's department and make a recommendation as to whether the department should be eliminated.

2. Prepare a projected income statement for Harrold's assuming the recommendation you provided in Requirement 1 is implemented.

3. Comment on the qualitative features that could affect the elimination decision.

P3. Form for Requirement 1

Segment	Men's
Net Income	$ (1,000)

P3. Form for Requirement 2

Income After Elimination	
Sales	
Cost of Goods Sold	
Sales Commissions	
Contribution Margin	
Store Rent and General Fixed Overhead Cost	
Store Manager's Salary	
Department Manager's Salary	
Advertising Expense	
Operating Income	
Lease Income	
Net Income	$ 19,000

P3. Form for Requirement 3

P4. The CoBo Taxi Company is considering the replacement of one of its taxies. The old taxi purchased three years ago at a cost of $24,000. Its current book value using straight-line amortization is $10,000 and operating expenses (gas, oil, tires, maintenance) are $8,000 per year. A replacement car would cost $26,000 and have a useful life of four years. The new car would require $4,000 per year in operating expenses. It has an expected salvage value of $6,000. The current disposal value of the old car is $10,000 and if kept four more years, its salvage value would be $2,000.

Required:
1. Determine the relevant cost of operating the old taxi.

2. Determine the relevant cost of operating the new taxi.

3. Provide a recommendation as to whether the old taxi should be replaced.

P4. Form for Requirement 1

Relevant Cost of Operating Old Taxi	
Total Relevant Cost	$40,000

P4. Form for Requirement 2

Relevant Cost of Operating New Taxi	
Total Relevant Cost	$36,000

P4. Form for Requirement 3

Solutions for Multiple Choice Problems

1. d

2. c The sales commission cost is not relevant because it will be paid regardless of whether the product is manufactured in house or is outsourced. Since the sales commission cost does not differ between the alternatives, it cannot be avoided and therefore is not relevant. Due to qualitative considerations it may be wise to continue manufacturing the calculator even if it costs less to purchases it. Therefor answer d is true.

3. c

4. a

5. c The product-level engineering and advertising costs will be the same regardless of whether the special order is accepted or rejected. Since these costs cannot be avoided by rejecting the special offer, they are not relevant to the decision.

6. b Since the unit-level costs and the cost of starting a new batch could be avoided if the special offer were rejected, these costs are relevant. Accordingly, the relevant cost of making 1,000 additional protectors is computed as follows:

Unit-Level		
Materials	$ 7.00 x 1,000 units	$ 7,000
Labour	$12.00 x 1,000 units	12,000
Overhead	$ 3.00 x 1,000 units	3,000
Batch-Level		4,000
Total		$26,000

Additional revenues are $24,000 ($24 x 1,000 units = $24,000). Accordingly, accepting the special order would decrease profitability by $2,000 ($24,000 revenue minus $26,000 relevant cost).

7. a Only the unit-level costs are relevant. Accordingly, the relevant cost is $15 ($5 material + $2 labour + $6 overhead + $2 selling). All other costs will be incurred regardless of whether the special offer is accepted or rejected. Since these costs do not differ between the alternatives, they are not relevant.

8. a The change in profitability is determined by the difference between the relevant (incremental) revenue minus the relevant (incremental) expenses that will result from the acceptance of the special offer. In this case, relevant revenue is $1,200,000 ($24 x 50,000 units). Relevant costs amount to $750,000 ($15 x 50,000). Accordingly, profitability will increase by $450,000 ($1,200,000 – $750,000) if the special offer is accepted.

9. d

10. c
Unit-level material	(600 x $45)	$ 27,000
Unit-level labour	(600 x $90)	54,000
Unit-level overhead	(600 x $30)	18,000
Opportunity cost		9,000
Total Relevant Cost		$108,000

Cost Per Unit = ($108,000 ÷ 600) = $180

11. b   Total Relevant Cost to Make $108,000   (600 x $180)
      Total Cost to Purchase   (121,500)   (600 x $202.50)
      Effect on net income   ($13,500)

   Since the cost of purchasing the components is more than the relevant cost of making them, net income would decrease if the components are purchased.

12. a   The cost to make is less than the cost to purchase. See above computations.

13. d

15. b

Old Equipment:		New Equipment:	
Opportunity Cost	29,000	Purchase Price	54,000
Operating Expenses	36,000	Salvage Value	(4,000)
		Operating Expenses	20,000
Relevant Cost of Old	65,000	Relevant Cost of New	70,000

   Since replacing the old equipment will cost $5,000 more than continuing to operate it, profitability will decrease if the equipment is replaced.

Solutions to Exercise Type Problems

P1. Solution for Requirement 1

Since the product- and facility-level costs will be incurred regardless of whether the special order is accepted or rejected, they are not relevant. The relevant costs are as follows:

Unit-Level		
Materials	$ 2.00 x 200,000 units	$ 400,000
Labour	$ 1.50 x 200,000 units	300,000
Overhead	$ 2.50 x 200,000 units	500,000
Total		$1,200,000

P1. Solution for Requirement 2

Additional revenues are $1,400,000 ($7 x 200,000 units = $1,400,000).

P1. Solution for Requirement 3

Accepting the special order would increase profitability by $200,000 ($1,400,000 revenue minus $1,200,000 relevant cost). Accordingly, the special order should be accepted.

P1. Solution for Requirement 4

If DDC's regular customers become aware that other customers are receiving lower prices, they may demand equal treatment. DDC's profitability would decline significantly, if the special order price of $7 per unit were extended to all customers. Accordingly, the special order should be rejected unless it can be completed without causing disruptions to DDC's existing customer base. In other words, the special order customers must be located outside DDC's normal territory.

P2. Solution for Requirement 1

Amortization is a sunk cost that is not relevant. Sales commissions, fixed selling cost, and the allocated portion of corporate level facility-level costs will be the same regardless of whether products made or bought. The remaining costs of production could be avoided, if the jackets were purchased. These costs are shown below:

Relevant Costs Associated with Making Life Jackets	
Cost of Materials (6,000 Units x $7)	$42,000
Labour (6,000 Units x $8)	48,000
Salary of Production Supervisor	30,000
Product-Level Legal Costs	24,000
Rental Cost of Equipment Used to Make Jackets	12,000
Total Relevant Cost to Make 6,000 Jackets	$156,000

P2. Solution for Requirement 2

The relevant cost of purchasing 6,000 jackets is $192,000 (6,000 units x $32 per unit)

P2. Solution for Requirement 3

Since the relevant cost to make the jackets is less than the cost to purchase them, SI should continue to make the jackets.

P2. Solution for Requirement 4

Since SI plans to sell the jackets regardless of whether the company makes the jackets or purchases them for resale, the selling costs will be incurred regardless of whether the jackets are outsourced. Since the selling costs cannot be avoided, they are not relevant.

P3. Solution for Requirement 1

The cost of store rent and general fixed overhead plus the cost of the store manager's salary will be incurred regardless of whether the men's department is eliminated. Since these costs are not avoidable, they are not relevant. Using the store space for the men's department forces Harrold's to give up the opportunity to receive lease income. This is an opportunity cost that is relevant to the elimination decision. The revenue and relevant cost of operating the men's department is shown below. Since the relevant cost exceed the revenue, the segment should be eliminated.

Segment	Men's
Sales	$107,000
Cost of Goods Sold	(74,000)
Sales Commissions	(12,000)
Contribution Margin	21,000
Department Manager's Salary	(6,000)
Advertising Expense	(5,000)
Opportunity Cost of Lease	(11,000)
Net Income	$ (1,000)

P3. Solution for Requirement 2

Income After Elimination	
Sales	$224,000
Cost of Goods Sold	(86,000)
Sales Commissions	(22,000)
Contribution Margin	116,000
Store Rent and General Fixed Overhead Cost	(70,000)
Store Manager's Salary	(20,000)
Department Manager's Salary	(8,000)
Advertising Expense	(10,000)
Operating Income	8,000
Lease Income	11,000
Net Income	$ 19,000

Notice that the after elimination net income figure confirms the conclusion reached in Requirement 1. Recall that the solution to Requirement 1 suggested that the men's department was generating a $1,000 loss for the company as a whole. This is confirmed by the data above which shows that the net income of the store as a whole rose from $18,000 to $19,000 when the men's department was eliminated.

P3. Solution for Requirement 3

There are several qualitative features that should be considered. Some of these include the possibility of interrelated sales between the men's and women's departments. For example, some of the women's sales may result from male customers who buy something for their spouse when they are purchasing items for themselves. These male customers may not enter the store if there is no men's department. Also, consideration should be given to the type of business the lessee plans to open. For example, the lessee could open a restaurant that generated an offensive odor. This condition could drive away customers from the women's department.

P4. Solution for Requirement 1

Relevant Cost of Operating Old Taxi	
Market Value	$10,000
Salvage Value	(2,000)
Operating Expense (4 x $8,000)	32,000
Total Relevant Cost	$40,000

P4. Solution for Requirement 2

Relevant Cost of Operating New Taxi	
Market Value	$26,000
Salvage Value	(6,000)
Operating Expense (4 x $4,000)	16,000
Total Relevant Cost	$36,000

P4. Solution for Requirement 3

Since the relevant cost of operating the new taxi ($36,000) is less than the relevant cost of operating the old taxi ($40,000), the old taxi should be replaced.

Chapter 5
Cost Accumulation, Tracing, and Allocation

Learning Objectives for the Chapter

The material in this chapter of the study guide is designed to facilitate your ability to:

- Understand the relationships among cost objects, cost drivers, and cost allocation.
- Distinguish between direct versus indirect cost.
- Appreciate the unique nature of the direct cost concept and understand the context sensitive nature of cost classification.
- Understand the mathematical procedures used to make allocations.
- Select appropriate cost drivers for making allocations under a variety of different circumstances.
- Understand the implications of cost behavior associated with making allocations.
- Understand the need to establish cost pools.
- Understand the allocation of common costs associated with joint products and by-products.
- Understand the allocation of common costs associated with joint products and by-products.
- Understand the association between cost allocation and relevance.
- Understand the allocation of service center costs to operating departments under the direct and step methods. (Appendix)

Brief Explanation of the Learning Objectives

Understand the relationships among cost objects, cost drivers, and cost allocation.

Accountants are frequently charged with the task of determining the cost of a certain thing. The thing for which the cost is being determined is called a **cost object**. Examples of cost objects include products, processes, departments, services, and activities. Some costs are incurred for the benefit of several different cost objects. For example, the salary paid to a supervisor may benefit several different departments. If you are trying to determine the cost of operating each department (i.e., the departments are the cost objects), the supervisor's salary must be divided up and parts of it assigned to each department. The dividing and assignment process is known as **cost allocation**. Determining the amount of a cost to be assigned to a cost object is frequently facilitated by the use of a cost driver. A **cost driver** is a factor that is logically linked to the incurrence of a cost. To illustrate, assume that the supervisor is paid by the hour. Under theses circumstances the number of hours spent in each department could be used to link the supervisor's salary with the cost of operating a department. Departments requiring more of the supervisor's time would assigned a greater portion of the supervisor's salary.

Distinguish between direct versus indirect cost.

Direct costs are costs that can be traced to cost objects in a cost-effective manner. To be cost-effective, the informational benefits obtained from tracing the cost must be greater than the economic sacrifice made to trace it. Indirect costs are costs than cannot be traced to a cost object in a cost-effective manner. Therefore, indirect costs are allocated rather than traced to cost objects.

Appreciate the unique nature of the direct cost concept and understand the context sensitive nature of cost classification.

The classification of a cost as direct versus indirect is independent of cost behavior. More specifically, whether a cost is classified as fixed or variable has nothing to do with whether it will be classified as direct or indirect. Indeed, the same exact cost can be classified as direct, indirect, fixed, or variable depending on the circumstances. For example, the salary of a manager of a Wal-Mart store is directly traceable to the particular store that he or she manages, but is not traceable to any particular department within that store. The cost is fixed relative to the number of customers coming into the store but would be variable relative to the number of stores operated by Wal-Mart. Accordingly, you must learn to interpret the circumstances rather than memorize definitions.

Understand the mathematical procedures used to make allocations.

Allocations can be accomplished in a two step process. To illustrate assume that $5,000 of utility cost must be divided between two departments. Since both departments use manufacturing equipment that draws heavily on electrical power, machine hours has been designated as the cost driver. Department A operated its equipment for a total of 400 hours while Department B operated its equipment for 600 hours. The allocation of the utility cost could be accomplished as follows:

Step 1 Compute the ***allocation rate*** by dividing the ***total cost to be allocated*** (i.e., $5,000 utility cost) by the ***cost driver*** (i.e., 400 + 600 = 1,000 machine hours). *Since the **cost driver** is the basis for the allocation process, it is sometimes called the **allocation base**. The result of the process is called the **allocation rate***. The computation is shown below:

Total Cost to be Allocated ÷ Cost Driver (i.e., Allocation Base) = Allocation Rate

$5,000 Utility Cost ÷ 1,000 Machine Hours = $5.00 Per Machine Hour

Step 2 Multiply the *allocation rate* by the *weight of the cost driver* (i.e., weight of the base) to determine the allocation per *cost object*. This computation is shown below:

Cost Object	Allocation Rate	x	No. of hours	=	Allocation Per Cost Object
Department A	$5.00	x	400	=	$2,000
Department B	$5.00	x	600	=	3,000
Total			1,000		$5,000

Select appropriate cost drivers for making allocations under a variety of different circumstances.

Frequently, more than one cost driver is linked to a cost object. For example, the use of indirect supplies can be linked to the use of direct materials or direct labour. Consider the construction of a house as an example. The more lumber (direct material) used the more nails (indirect material) needed to attach it together. Similarly, the more direct labour used in the process of hammering nails, the more nails used. So which (direct materials or direct labour) is the best cost driver? The best cost driver is the one with the strongest cause-and-effect relationship. Since the workers may be involved in activities other than driving nails, the number of labour hours is not as closely related to the consumption of nails as is the amount of lumber used. Accordingly, material dollars would probably be a better cost driver than labour hours. As this example suggests, the selection of the best cost driver requires logic and good judgment.

Understand the implications of cost behavior associated with making allocations.

As previously indicated, indirect costs may exhibit variable or fixed cost behavior patterns. There is a causal relationship between the incurrence of variable overhead costs (e.g., indirect materials, inspection costs, utilities, etc.) and the volume of production. More specifically, increases in the volume of production will cause variable overhead costs to increase. In other words, volume drives the incurrence of the cost. For example, the cost of indirect materials such as glue, staples, screws, nails, and varnish will increase in proportion to the number of units of furniture made by a manufacturing company. Under these circumstances the number of units, labour hours, material dollars or some other volume measure would serve as good cost driver for the allocation of variable overhead costs. Fixed costs present a unique problem with respect to cost allocation. By definition there are no volume based cost drivers for a fixed cost (i.e., the cost stays the same regardless of the volume of activity). Even so, we may choose to use a volume based cost driver as the allocation base. The objective of allocating fixed costs to products is to distribute a fair share of the overhead cost to each product. In many instances a fair share distribution can be accomplished by selecting an allocation base that spreads the total overhead cost equally over the total volume of production. For example, number of units may be used to spread overhead cost evenly over the volume of production.

Understand the need to establish cost pools.

Allocating every single indirect cost that a company incurs would be a tedious and time-consuming task. To reduce the computational process, organizations frequently accumulate many individual costs into a single total called a **cost pool**. The total cost pool is then allocated to the cost objects. Accordingly, a single allocation can replace numerous allocations that would otherwise be required to distribute each individual cost to the relevant cost objects. For example, a company may accumulate the costs for phones, gas, water, and electricity into a single cost pool called utilities cost. The total cost in the utilities cost pool would then be allocated to the cost objects rather than making an individual allocation for each of the four types of utility cost.

Understand the allocation of common costs associated with joint products and by-products.

Joint costs are common costs that are incurred in the process of making two or more products. An example is the cost of raw milk (i.e., joint cost) that is used to make cream, whole milk, 2% milk, and skim milk. The products that are derived from joint costs are called joint products. The point in the production process where products become separate and identifiable is called the **split-off point**. For balance sheet valuation and income determination, all costs incurred up to the split-off point must be allocated to the joint products. Some products require additional processing after the split-off point. These separate and identifiable costs should be assigned to the specific products that cause their incurrence.

Understand the association between cost allocation and relevance.

Use caution when determining the relevance of allocated costs for decision making purposes. Many allocated costs will be incurred regardless of whatever action management takes. For example, allocated joint costs will continue to be incurred even if one of the joint products is eliminated.

Self-Study Problems

Multiple Choice Problems

1. Federated Department Stores is attempting to determine the cost of operating a particular store. Which of the following costs would be classified as an indirect cost?
   a. cost of goods sold
   b. salary of store manager
   c. cost of operating Federated's company airplane. *(circled)*
   d. supplies used by employees working in the men's department.

2. Depending on the circumstances the cost of employee compensation could be classified as a:
   a. product cost
   b. indirect cost
   c. relevant cost
   d. all of the above. *(circled)*

3. Allocation is used to assign costs to:
   a. cost objects *(circled)*
   b. cost drivers
   c. cost pools
   d. all of the above

4. What is the formula for determining the allocation rate?
   a. (total cost to be allocated)/(cost driver) *(circled)*
   b. (cost driver)/(total cost to be allocated)
   c. (allocation rate)/(cost driver)
   d. (cost driver-allocation rate)/(total cost to be allocated)

5. Select the most appropriate allocation base and determine the amount of this month's $3,600 office rental payment to Department C.

Department	Number of Employees	Square Metres
A	24	6,000
B	16	3,000
C	10	9,000
Total	50	18,000

   a. $1,200
   b. $1,800 *(circled)*
   c. $3,600
   d. $1,000

   Handwritten notes: → is the appropriate allocation

   $3,600 ÷ 50 = $72.00

   $3,600 ÷ 18,000 = $0.20

   Dept C
   Empl. 10 × $72.00 = $720.00
   Sq Mtr 9000 × .20 = $1800.00

6. The Baltic Company expects to incur $4,000 per month of fixed overhead costs during the first three months of the year, and $10 per unit of variable overhead costs. Expected production for January, February, and March is 4,000, 5,000 and 3,000, respectively. Based on this information, the pre-determined overhead rate for the first three months of the year is:
   a. $0.80 per unit
   b. $11.00 per unit
   c. $10.00 per unit
   d. $0.33 per unit

7. A factor having a "cause and effect" relationship with a cost object is called a:
   a. joint product
   b. relevant cost
   c. cost driver
   d. indirect cost

8. Production workers at Ditzel Manufacturing Company provided 1,400 hours of labour in January and 1,100 hours in February. Ditzel expects to use 15,600 hours of labour during the year and expects to pay an annual insurance premium of $39,000 sometime in March. How much of the insurance cost should be allocated to products made in January and to those made in February?

	January	February
a.	$2,000;	$5,500
b.	$3,500;	$1,250
c.	$4,000;	$1,750
d.	$3,500;	$2,750

9. Go Green Company expects to incur $133,000 of fringe benefits cost during the next accounting period. The company produces two types of products known a Compound A and Compound B. Making a unit of Compound A requires 5 hours of labour. Making a unit of Compound B requires 9 hours of labour. The company expects to make 500 units of one product and 900 units of the other product. Each unit of both products is expected to require $70 of raw materials cost. Which of the following statements is true? Total direct labour hours are expected to be 26,600.
   a. Number of units of product would be the most appropriate allocation base for the fringe benefits cost.
   b. The predetermined overhead rate for the fringe benefits cost should be $95 per unit.
   c. The predetermined overhead rate for the fringe benefits cost should be $5 per direct labour hour.
   d. a & b.

10. Based on the following history of production information, which allocation base would you choose to use for your company (i.e., what is the cost driver)?

	19X1	19X2	19X3
Units Produced	20,000	40,000	80,000
Dir. Labour Hours	15,000	12,000	10,000
Dir. Material Costs	$140,000	$130,000	$120,000 $390,000
Actual Overhead Costs	$40,000	$80,000 c	$160,000

a. Direct Material Costs
b. Units
c. Direct Labour Hours
d. All three bases materials cost, labour hours, or units would be equally appropriate

11. Which of the following is the least logical cost driver for allocating indirect materials cost to three custom build houses that are different with respect to size?
a. square metres of floor space
b. direct labour hours
(c.) number of houses
d. expected sales price measured in dollars

12. ABC Company uses a cost plus pricing strategy. ABC uses a predetermined overhead rate to allocate fixed manufacturing overhead cost to production on a monthly basis. At the end of the accounting period it was determined that actual overhead cost was more than the estimated overhead cost; however, the actual volume of production was exactly as expected. Based on this information alone:
a. products were overpriced during the accounting period.
b. products were priced accurately during the accounting period.
c. products were underpriced during the accounting period.
d. the answer cannot be determined from the information provided.

Use the following information to answer the next three questions:
Gilbert Manufacturing makes two products, Zeon and Halo. They are processed from the same material initially and then, after split off, Zeon is further processed separately. Additional information is as follows:

	Zion	Halo
Units Produced and Sold	180 Units	60 Units
Unit Selling Price at Split-off	$1200	$600
Additional Cost if Processed Further	$30,000	
Unit Selling Price After Additional Processing	$1,400	
Joint Costs		$108,864

13. The joint costs allocated to each product using the number of units produced and sold would be:

	Zion	Halo
a.	$81,648	$27,216
b.	$30,000	$78,864
c.	$72,864	$36,000
d.	$93,312	$15,552

14. The joint cost allocated to Zion using the sales value at the split-off point would be:
    a. $81,648
    b. $93,312
    c. $15,552
    d. $17,143

15. If Zion is further processed, profitability would change by what amount?
    a. ($6,000)
    b. ($36,000)
    c. $36,000
    d. $6,000

Exercise Type Problems

P1. Choi Chemical Company operates four divisions. The amount of floor space used by each division is shown below:

Division	Square Metres
North	4,000
East	5,000
South	7,000
West	2,000
Total	18,000

Choi's annual building rental cost is $270,000.

Required: Determine the amount of the rental cost that should be allocated to each division.

P1. Form for Problem 1

Step1: Determine the allocation Rate:

Step2: Determine the cost to be allocated:

Cost Object	Allocation Rate	x	No. of Square Metres	=	Allocation Per Cost Object
Total		x	18,000	=	$270,000

P2. Graham Manufacturing Company (GMC) has divided its manufacturing operations in two departments. Department A is an assembly department. The assembly department uses robotic equipment to construct the company's products. Department B is a packaging and shipping department. This department is labour intensive and requires a large number of workers to prepare the products for delivery. The total overhead cost amounts to $240,000. This cost can be subdivided into two major components including $90,000 of fringe benefits and $150,000 of utility costs. The expected machine and labour hour consumption patterns for the two departments are as follows:

	Machine Hours	Labour Hours
Department A	27,000	6,000
Department B	3,000	14,000
Total	30,000	20,000

GMC places great emphasis on the control of cost. Managers who are able to minimize their department's cost are rewarded with bonuses.

Required:
1. Identify the cost driver (machine hours or labour hours) that will assign the least amount of overhead cost to Department A. Using this cost driver allocate the total overhead cost to the two departments.

2. Identify the cost driver (machine hours or labour hours) that will assign the least amount of overhead cost to Department B. Using this cost driver allocate the total overhead cost to the two departments.

3. Formulate an overhead allocation policy that would be fair to the supervisors of both Department A and Department B. Compute the overhead allocations for each department using your policy.

P2. Form for Requirement 1

Total Cost to be Allocated ÷ Cost Driver (i.e., Allocation Base) = Allocation Rate

Cost Object	Allocation Rate	x	No. of Labour Hours	=	Allocation Per Cost Object
Total	$12	x	20,000	=	$240,000

P2. Form for Requirement 2

Total Cost to be Allocated ÷ Cost Driver (i.e., Allocation Base) = Allocation Rate

Cost Object	Allocation Rate	x	No. of Machine Hours	=	Allocation Per Cost Object
Total	$8	x	30,000	=	$240,000

P2. Form for Requirement 3

Using labour hours as the cost driver for fringe benefits will produce the following cost allocations for the two Departments:

Total Cost to be Allocated ÷ Cost Driver (i.e., Allocation Base) = Allocation Rate

Cost Object	Allocation Rate	x	No. of Labour Hours	=	Allocation Per Cost Object
Total	$4.50	x	20,000	=	$90,000

Using machine hours as the cost driver for utility cost will produce the following cost allocations for the two Departments:

Total Cost to be Allocated ÷ Cost Driver (i.e., Allocation Base) = Allocation Rate

Cost Object	Allocation Rate	x	No. of Machine Hours	=	Allocation Per Cost Object
Total	$5	x	30,000	=	$150,000

The total overhead allocation for the two Departments is shown below:

Cost Object	Fringe Benefits Cost	+	Utility Cost	=	Total Overhead Allocation
Total	$90,000	+	$150,000	=	$240,000

P3. Fairfield Corporation manufactures products C and D from a single process. Joint costs including materials and processing costs totaled $69,600. Joint costs are allocated on the basis of relative sales value at split-off. Additional information is as follows:

Products	C	D
Litres Produced	1,500	1,800
Sales Value at Split-off	$40,000	$80,000

Required:
1. Using the sales value at the split-off point as the allocation base (cost driver), determine the amount of the joint cost that should be allocated to each product. Also, determine the gross margin for each product.

2. Assume that a change in government regulations will require additional processing costs of $25,000 for Product C. After the additional processing, Product C will have a sales value of $45,000. Determine the gross margin for Product C. Based on this information, should Fairfield discontinue the production of Product C?

P3. Form for Requirement 1

Total Cost to be Allocated ÷ Cost Driver (i.e., Allocation Base) = Allocation Rate

Cost Object	Allocation Rate	x	No. of Sales Dollars	=	Allocation Per Cost Object
Total	$0.58	x	120,000	=	$69,600

Determination of Gross Margin

	Product C	Product D
Revenue		
Joint Cost		
Gross Margin	16,800	33,600

P3. Form for Requirement 2

Determination of Gross Margin

	Product C
Revenue	
Joint Cost	
Gross Margin	
Additional Processing Cost	
Gross Margin	(8,200)

Should Fairfield discontinue the production of Product C?

Multiple Choice Problems - Solutions

1. c Since the plane is operated for the benefit of the company as a whole, it cannot be directly traced to any particular store.

2. d If the compensation were direct labour of a production worker it would be a product cost. If the cost were for a production supervisor working in many departments the cost would not be directly traceable (would be indirect) to any particular department. If the cost differed between two decision alternatives it would be relevant to a choice between the alternatives. Other examples are possible, but these confirm the fact that the cost could be classified into any of the categories named in choices a, b, and c.

3. a Answer "b" is incorrect because cost drivers are used as the basis for allocation, rather than the result of it. Answere "c" is incorrect because costs are pooled and then allocated rather than allocated into pools.

4. a

5. b Total Cost to be Allocated ÷ Cost Driver (i.e., Allocation Base) = Allocation Rate

    $3,600 Rental Cost ÷ 18,000 Square Metres = $0.20 Per Square Foot

Cost Object	Allocation Rate	x	No. of Square Metres	=	Allocation Per Cost Object
Department C	$0.20	x	9,000	=	$1,800

6. b Total Estimated Cost to be Allocated ÷ Allocation Base = Predetermined OH Rate

    [($4,000 x 3) + ($10 x 12,000 Units)] ÷ 12,000 Units = $11 Per Unit

7. c

8. d Total Cost to be Allocated ÷ Cost Driver (i.e., Allocation Base) = Allocation Rate

    $39,000 Premium ÷ 15,600 Hours = $2.50 Per Hour

Cost Object	Allocation Rate	x	No. of Hours	=	Allocation Per Cost Object
January	$2.50	x	1,400	=	$3,500
February	$2.50	x	1,100	=	$2,750

9. c The most rational allocation base (cost driver) for the fringe benefits cost is labour hours.

    Total Estimated Cost to be Allocated ÷ Allocation Base = Predetermined OH Rate

    $133,000 fringe benefits cost ÷ 26,600 Hours = $5.00 Per Hour

10. b The data suggest that there is a cause and effect relationship between units produced and the actual overhead cost. Indeed, overhead cost is consistently twice as large as the number of units. Neither material cost nor labour hours have a consistent relationship with overhead cost.

11. c Using the number of houses as the allocation base would assign the same amount of overhead cost to each house. This would be inappropriate because the sizes of the houses are different, thereby suggesting that different amounts of indirect materials would be used on the different houses.

12. c   If actual overhead was more than expected, an insufficient amount of overhead was allocated to the products. Since the products were under costed, they would also have been under priced.

13. a   Total Cost to be Allocated ÷ Cost Driver (i.e., Allocation Base) = Allocation Rate

$108,864 Joint Cost ÷ 240 Units = $453.60 Per Unit

Cost Object	Allocation Rate	x	No. of Units	=	Allocation Per Cost Object
Zion	$453.60	x	180	=	$ 81,648
Halo	$453.60	x	60		27,216
Total					$108,864

14. b

Sales Price	x	No. of Units	=	Sales Value
$1,200	x	180	=	$216,000
$600	x	60		36,000
Total Sales Value				$252,000

Total Cost to be Allocated ÷ Cost Driver (i.e., Allocation Base) = Allocation Rate

$108,864 Joint Cost ÷ $252,000 Sales Value = $0.432 Per Dollar

Cost Object	Allocation Rate	x	Sales Value	=	Allocation Per Cost Object
Zion	$0.432	x	216,000	=	$ 93,312

15. d

Price After Additional Processing	$1,400
Price Before Additional Processing	(1,200)
Change in Sales Price	$200
Times Number of Units	x 180
Incremental Sales Revenue	$36,000
Additional Processing Cost	30,000
Change in Net Income	$6,000

Exercise Type Problems - Solutions

P1. Solution

Step1: Determine the allocation Rate:

Total Cost to be Allocated ÷ Cost Driver (i.e., Allocation Base) = Allocation Rate

$270,000 Rental Cost ÷ 18,000 Square Metres = $15 Per Square Foot

Step2: Determine the cost to be allocated:

Cost Object	Allocation Rate	x	No. of Square Metres	=	Allocation Per Cost Object
North	$15	x	4,000	=	$60,000
East	$15	x	5,000	=	75,000
South	$15	x	7,000	=	105,000
West	$15	x	2,000	=	30,000
Total	$15	x	18,000	=	$270,000

P2. Solution for Requirement 1

Since Department A uses less labour hours than Department B, the use of labour hours as the cost driver will minimize the amount of cost allocated to Department A. The amount of cost allocated to each department would be as follows:

Total Cost to be Allocated ÷ Cost Driver (i.e., Allocation Base) = Allocation Rate
$240,000 Overhead Cost ÷ 20,000 Labour Hours = $12 Per Labour Hour

Cost Object	Allocation Rate	x	No. of Labour Hours	=	Allocation Per Cost Object
Department A	$12	x	6,000	=	$ 72,000
Department B	$12	x	14,000	=	168,000
Total	$12	x	20,000	=	$240,000

P2. Solution for Requirement 2

Since Department B uses less machine hours than Department A, the use of machine hours as the cost driver will minimize the amount of cost allocated to Department B. The amount of cost allocated to each department would be as follows:

Total Cost to be Allocated ÷ Cost Driver (i.e., Allocation Base) = Allocation Rate
$240,000 Overhead Cost ÷ 30,000 Machine Hours = $8 Per Machine Hour

Cost Object	Allocation Rate	x	No. of Machine Hours	=	Allocation Per Cost Object
Department A	$8	x	27,000	=	$ 216,000
Department B	$8	x	3,000	=	24,000
Total	$8	x	30,000	=	$240,000

P2. Solution for Requirement 3

There is a logical link between labour hours and fringe benefits. Also, there is a logical link between machine hours and utility cost. Accordingly, a more rational allocation can be accomplished by using different cost drivers for the two types of overhead cost.

Using labour hours as the cost driver for fringe benefits will produce the following cost allocations for the two Departments:

Total Cost to be Allocated ÷ Cost Driver (i.e., Allocation Base) = Allocation Rate
$90,000 Fringe Benefits Cost ÷ 20,000 Labour Hours = $4.50 Per Labour Hour

Cost Object	Allocation Rate	x	No. of Labour Hours	=	Allocation Per Cost Object
Department A	$4.50	x	6,000	=	$27,000
Department B	$4.50	x	14,000	=	63,000
Total	$4.50	x	20,000	=	$90,000

Using machine hours as the cost driver for utility cost will produce the following cost allocations for the two Departments:

Total Cost to be Allocated ÷ Cost Driver (i.e., Allocation Base) = Allocation Rate
$150,000 Utility Cost ÷ 30,000 Machine Hours = $5 Per Machine Hour

Cost Object	Allocation Rate	x	No. of Machine Hours	=	Allocation Per Cost Object
Department A	$5	x	27,000	=	$ 135,000
Department B	$5	x	3,000	=	15,000
Total	$5	x	30,000	=	$150,000

The total overhead allocation for the two Departments is shown below:

Cost Object	Fringe Benefits Cost	+	Utility Cost	=	Total Overhead Allocation
Department A	$27,000	+	$ 135,000	=	$ 162,000
Department B	63,000	+	15,000	=	78,000
Total	$90,000	+	$150,000	=	$240,000

P3. Solution for Requirement 1

Total Cost to be Allocated ÷ Cost Driver (i.e., Allocation Base) = Allocation Rate
$69,600 Joint Cost ÷ 120,000 Sales Value = $0.58 Per Machine Hour

Cost Object	Allocation Rate	x	No. of Sales Dollars	=	Allocation Per Cost Object
Product C	$0.58	x	$40,000	=	$23,200
Product D	$0.58	x	80,000	=	46,400
Total	$0.58	x	120,000	=	$69,600

Determination of Gross Margin

	Product C	Product D
Revenue A	40,000	80,000
Joint Costs	(23,200)	(46,400)
Gross Margin	16,800	33,600

P3. Solution for Requirement 2

	Product C
Revenue	45,000
Joint Cost	(23,200)
Gross Margin	21,800
Additional Processing Cost	(25,000)
Gross Margin	(3,200)

Assuming that Product D will continue to be produced, the $23,200 of joint cost allocated to Product C would not be relevant to the additional processing decision because the joint cost will be incurred regardless of whether the additional processing is undertaken. With respect to Product C, you must compare the required additional processing cost of $25,000 with the $45,000 of revenue that will result from the sell of that product. Since the revenue exceeds the additional processing cost, Fairfield should undertake the additional processing in order to continue the production of Product C.

Chapter 6

Cost Management in an Automated Business Environment (ABC, ABM, and TQM)

Learning Objectives for the Chapter

The material in this chapter of the study guide is designed to facilitate your ability to:

- Understand the limitations associated with using direct labour hours as a single company-wide overhead allocation rate.
- Understand how automation has affected the selection of cost drivers.
- Distinguish between volume-based versus activity-based cost drivers.
- Identify and use activity cost centers and related costs drivers in an activity-based cost system.
- Classify activities into one of four hierarchical categories including unit-level, batch-level, product-level, and facility-level activities.
- Understand the effect under or over costing can have on profitability.
- Distinguish between manufacturing, upstream, and downstream costs.
- Appreciate the limitations of activity-based costing including the effects of employee attitudes and the availability of data.
- Categorize quality costs into one of four categories including: prevention cost, appraisal cost, internal failure cost, and external failure cost.
- Understand relationships between the components of quality cost.
- Prepare and interpret information contained in quality cost reports.

Brief Explanation of the Learning Objectives

Understand the limitations associated with using direct labour hours as a single company-wide overhead allocation rate

Traditionally, companies accumulated all overhead costs into one cost pool and then used direct labour hours as the sole basis for allocating that cost pool to cost objects. Unfortunately, many of today's overhead costs cannot be logically linked to direct labour usage. For example, products that are made with robotics may have significant utility and depreciation costs that are not related to direct labour usage. If direct labour hours is used as the sole cost driver, the overhead costs such as these will be misallocated.

Understand how automation has affected the selection of cost drivers.

Automation has shifted the workload from human labour to mechanical production. As a result, labour usage may not be related to the incurrence of significant overhead costs such as utilities and depreciation. A flip of an on and off switch (human labour) can result in the manufacture of any number of products. In other words, the amount of human labour is not related to the volume of production. Indeed, many other costs may not be related to the volume of production. For example, set up costs may be high for a product made in low volume and low for a product made in high volume. In a effort to improve the accuracy of allocations, accountants have begun to pool costs according to the activities (e.g. costs associated with setup activities) that caused those overhead costs to be incurred. A variety of cost drivers (as opposed to a single company-wide allocation base) is then used to allocate the activity-based cost pools to the cost objects.

Distinguish between volume-based versus activity-based cost drivers

Volume-based cost drivers are linked to the level of production. In other words, the amount of these cost drivers increase or decrease consistent with changes in the level of production. For example, the cost of direct materials increases or decreases as the level of production (number of units of a product) increases or decreases. Other examples of volume based cost drivers include labour hours, labour dollars, material quantities, material dollars, and number of units. Activity-based cost drivers are linked to the level of activity. The amount of activity-based cost drivers changes with the level of activity. Examples of activity-based cost drivers include number of setups, number of service requests, number of inspections, etc.

Identify and use activity cost centers and related costs drivers in an activity-based cost system.

Activities are actions taken by an organization to accomplish its mission. Many different activities have similar characteristics. For example, activities associated with the design of a product, obtaining a patent, and establishing a brand name are all associated with developing a particular product. The activities that have similar characteristics are frequently pooled into a single unit know as an activity center. The costs of operating the activity center are then allocated using a single cost driver. Accordingly, activity cost centers reduce the number of allocations that are necessary to determine the cost of designated objects.

Classify activities into one of four hierarchical categories including unit-level, batch-level, product-level, and facility-level activities

Definitions of the four categories are as follows:

a. **Unit-level activities** increase or decrease each time a unit of product is added or subtracted from the production process. Examples include activities associated with direct labour and or per unit inspections.

b. **Batch-level activities** increase or decrease each time a batch is added or subtracted from the production process. Examples include activities associated setting up and testing for quality control.

c. **Product-level activities** increase or decrease each time a product or product-line is added or subtracted from the production process. Examples include legal and engineering services associated with a particular product. The distinguishing feature here is between different products versus more units of the same product.

d. **Facility-level activities** increase or decrease each time a new facility is added or an existing facility is eliminated. Examples include factory maintenance and administrative activities.

Understand the effect that under or over costing can have on profitability

Under costing (i.e., allocated cost is lower than actual cost) can lead to pricing products at a lower amount than should be charged. The lower prices reduce profitability. In extreme cases products can even be priced below cost thereby resulting in losses. Over costing (allocated cost is higher than actual cost) can lead to prices that are not competitive thereby resulting in a decline in market share and profitability. Accordingly, the accuracy of allocations is critically important to the profitability of an enterprise.

Appreciate the limitations of activity-based costing including the effects of employee attitudes and the availability of data

The ultimate goal of activity-based costing is increased efficiency which frequently manifests itself in the elimination of non-value added activities. This can lead to the loss of jobs for employees. Accordingly, employees may be reluctant to cooperate in the implementation of an activity based cost system unless they are given assurances that they will not become victims of their own success. Also, activity-based costing can be diminished by the lack of data. For example, allocating the cost of inspections by the number of inspections performed cannot be accomplished if information regarding the number of inspections is not available.

Categorize quality costs into one of four categories including: prevention cost, appraisal cost, internal failure cost, and external failure cost.

Prevention and appraisal costs are incurred because of the potential for a lack of conformance with quality standards. **Prevention costs** are made to avoid nonconforming products. **Appraisal costs** are incurred to identify nonconforming products that were not avoided via the prevention cost expenditures. Failure costs result from the actual occurrence of nonconforming events. **Internal failure costs** are incurred when defects are corrected before the goods reach the customer. **External failure costs** occur when defective goods are delivered to customers.

Understand relationships between the components of quality cost.

The four components can be summarized into two broad categories. Since prevention and appraisal costs are a function of managerial discretion, they are often called **voluntary costs**. Management makes direct decisions as to the amount of funds to be expended for these voluntary costs. In contrast, **failure costs** are not directly controllable by management. For example, the cost of customer dissatisfaction may not be measurable much less controllable. Even though failure cost may not be directly controllable, they are definitely related to voluntary costs. When additional funds are allocated for prevention and appraisal activities, failure costs tend to decline. The logic is obvious. As the level of control increases, quality conformance increases thereby lowering failure costs. When control activities are reduced, quality conformance decreases and failure cost increase. Accordingly, *voluntary costs and failure costs move in opposite directions*.

Prepare and interpret information contained in quality cost reports

Managing quality costs in a manner that leads to the highest level of customer satisfaction is known as **total quality management (TQM)**. To facilitate TQM management accountants are frequently asked to prepare a **quality cost report**. This report typically lists the company's quality costs and provides a vertical analysis showing each item as a percentage of the total cost. Data is normally shown for two or more accounting periods in order to reveal the effects of changes over time.

Self-Study Problems

Multiple Choice Problems

Use the following information to answer the next two questions:
After its facilities were automated, Merryweather Metal Works was able to reduce labour hours for Product A by 3,000 hours. Before automation, Product A consumed 8,000 labour hours. Product B was not affected by the automation and continued to consume 7,000 labour hours. Automation increased total overhead from $30,000 to $36,000.

1. Which of the following choices would be true about the amount of overhead allocation if labour hours is used as the company-wide allocation base?

	Product	Before Automation	After Automation
a.	A	$24,000	$15,000
b.	B	$14,000	$14,000
c.	B	$21,000	$14,000
d.	A	$16,000	$15,000

2. Which of the following statements is true with regard to the amount of overhead allocation if the company continues to use direct labour hours as the cost driver?
   a. After automation, Product A is under costed.
   b. After automation Product A is over costed.
   c. After automation Product B is over costed.
   d. Both a and c.

3. Beeline Company produces two kinds of porch furniture, wicker and wrought iron. The company uses a company-wide allocation rate, direct labour hours, to assign overhead to its products. Through market research, the company has learned that the wrought iron furniture is not selling due to its high selling price. Beeline employs a cost plus pricing policy. Both types of furniture require the same number of direct labour hours, but the wicker furniture requires more machine set-ups and more expensive packaging. Which of the following options is most reasonable?
   a. Emphasize the sales of wicker furniture
   b. Use activity based costing and adjust prices accordingly
   c. Use number of units rather than direct labour hours as the allocation base
   d. Eliminate the wrought iron furniture from the company's furniture line

4. Which of the following costs would be most fairly allocated using a volume based cost driver?
   a. rental costs of manufacturing facility
   b. advertising cost for a product line
   c. indirect materials costs
   d. inspection costs for product batches

Use the following information to answer the next five question:
Jesob Company produces two automotive parts, carbulators and air filters. Both products are made in the same manufacturing facilities but are produced under different processes. To accomplish an accurate allocation of production costs, the company uses activity based costing. The cost accountant for the company provided information about the activities used to produce the company's products. The activities were organized into the following overhead cost categories. The most appropriate cost driver for each category is also provided.

Category	Estimated Cost	Cost Driver	Carburetors	Air Filters
Unit-Level	$60,000	Labour Hours	900	700
Batch-Level	$22,000	Set-ups	20	30
Product-Level	$45,000	Storage Space	2,000 sq metres	4,000 sq. metres
Facility-Level	$100,000	Machine Hours	7,500	12,500

5. The amount of batch-level cost that should be allocated to the carburetor product line would be:
   a. $13,200
   b. $9,625
   c. $14,250
   d. $8,800

6. The amount of facility-level cost that should be assigned to air filters is:
   a. $62,500
   b. $37,500
   c. $100,000
   d. none of the above

7. If carburetors and air filters require the same amount of direct labour, using labour hours as the allocation base for product-level costs would act to …
   a. Air filters will be over costed
   b. Carburetors will be over costed
   c. Air Filters and carburetors will be under costed
   d. The answer cannot be determined from the information provided

8. Assuming activity based costing is used, which of the following statements are true?
   a. more unit-level cost will be assigned to air filters.
   b. more batch-level cost will be assigned to carburetors.
   c. more product-level cost will be assigned to air filters.
   d. more facility-level cost will be assigned to carburetors.

9. Which of the following costs is the result of a facility-level activity?
   a. setup costs for a batch of work
   b. the cost of maintaining security for the manufacturing building
   c. the direct labour costs
   d. advertising costs for one of the company's products

10. By increasing the costs of prevention and appraisal activities, a company could expect…
    a. an increase in customer dissatisfaction with product quality.
    b. improvement in the quality image of its product.
    c. an increase in external failure costs.
    d. a decrease in quality control.

11. Which of the following quality costs are directly controllable by management?
    a. external failure costs
    b. internal failure costs
    c. appraisal costs
    d. all of the above

12. If one were to graph the voluntary costs and the failure costs of quality control, one would expect…
    a. the two costs to move in opposite directions.
    b. the two costs to move in the same direction.
    c. the two costs to be parallel.
    d. the two costs to be perpendicular.

13. The minimum total quality cost is at the point…
    a. of zero defects.
    b. at the lowest amount of prevention and appraisal costs.
    c. where marginal assurance cost (voluntary cost) equal marginal saving on failure cost.
    d. at the lowest level of costs for correcting defects before they reach the customer.

Exercise Type Problems

P1. Finn Company makes two types of weight-lifting equipment. One is a rowing machine; the other is a stationary bicycle. For years, Finn's operations were so small that the employment of automated techniques was not cost effective. The company was heavily dependent on manual labour to make its products. However, demand for the bicycle had recently reached a level that enabled Finn to automate its production. The shift from manual labour to mechanical equipment is evident in the following before and after automation data.

Labour Hours	Before	After
Bicycle	80,000	30,000
Rower	20,000	20,000
Total	100,000	50,000

Machine Hours	Before	After
Bicycle	16,000	40,000
Rower	4,000	4,000
Total	20,000	44,000

Finn incurred $90,000 in utility cost prior to the automation. The utility cost increased to $220,000 after automation. Prior to automation, Finn used direct labour hours as a single company-wide overhead rate.

Required:

1. Determine the amount of utility cost that would be allocated to bicycles and rowers before and after automation assuming Finn continues to use direct labour hours as the cost driver (i.e., allocation base) after automation. Notice that while labour hours used in the production of rowers remained constant, the amount of utility cost allocated to this product increased dramatically after automation. Explain why this phenomenon occurs.

2. Determine the amount of utility cost that would be allocated to bicycles and rowers assuming Finn uses direct labour hours before automation and machine hours after automation.

3. Comment on the use of machine hours as an allocation bases after automation. Should machine hours be used for the allocation of all overhead cost? Explain your answer.

P1. Form for Requirement 1

	Before Automation	After Automation
Overhead Rate		
Allocated Cost		
Bikes		
Rowers		

Comments:

P1. Form for Requirement 2

	Before Automation	After Automation
Overhead Rate		
Allocated Cost		
Bikes		
Rowers		

P1. Form for Requirement 3

Comments:

P2. Haberman Company is considering the possibility of implementing an activity based cost (ABC) system. At this point the company uses direct labour hours as a company-wide overhead allocation base to allocate the total overhead costs amounting to $810,000. Haberman's accountant collected the following information to help evaluate the potential benefits of an ABC system.

Activities	Unit-level	Batch-level	Product-level	Facility-level
Annual Cost	$360,000	$288,000	$93,000	$69,000
Cost Driver	300,000 Labour hours	240 Set ups	% of Use	60,000 Square metres

Haberman makes 18 different types of small tools. The company's hammer sells the best. Its wrench is its slowest moving product. It requires approximately 15 minutes of labour to make a hammer and 15 minutes of labour to make a wrench. Both hammers and wrenches require 12 machine set-ups per year. However, hammers are made in batches of 10,000 units while wrenches are made in batches of 1,000 units. Each of the two products uses approximately 10% of the product level costs. The production facilities devoted to hammers is approximate 3,000 square metres. An equal amount of square metres of space is devoted to the production of wrenches.

Required:
1. Explain why using direct labour hours as a company wide allocation rate creates inaccuracies in the amount of cost allocated to hammers versus wrenches.

2. Haberman uses a cost plus pricing system. If direct labour hours are used as a company wide allocation rate, will hammers or wrenches be over priced? Explain your answer.

3. Determine the amount of overhead cost allocated to hammers and to wrenches and the allocated cost per unit for hammers and for wrenches, if activity based costing is implemented.

P2. Form for Requirement 1

Comments:

P2. Form for Requirement 2

Comments:

P2. Form for Requirement 3

Allocation for Hammers

Cost	Cost ÷ Driver	Allocation = Rate	Weight x of Base	Allocated Cost
Total Allocated Cost				$63,150

Cost Per Unit for Hammers:

Allocation for Wrenches:

Cost	Cost ÷ Driver	Allocation = Rate	Weight x of Base	Allocated Cost
Total Allocated Cost				$30,750

Cost Per Unit for Wrenches:

P3. The following quality cost report was drawn from the records of Harris Company

	20X3		20X2	
	Amount	Percentage	Amount	Percentage
Prevention Costs:	200,000	11.8	500,000	38.5
Appraisal Costs:	200,000	11.8	300,000	23.1
Internal Failure Costs:	700,000	41.2	200,000	15.4
External Failure Cost	600,000	35.3	300,000	23.1
Grand Total*	1,700,000	100.0*	1,300,000	100.0*

*Percentages do not total exactly due to rounding.

Required: Based on the information contained in the quality cost report, speculate as to Harris' strategy for controlling total quality cost. Comment on the effectiveness of Harris' strategy for controlling total quality cost.

P3. Form for Requirement

Comments:

Solutions for Multiple Choice Problems

1. d

	Before Automation	After Automation
Product A	8,000 hours	5,000 hours
Product B	7,000 hours	7,000 hours
Total	15,000 hours	12,000 hours

   Overhead Rate $30,000 ÷ 15,000 = $2 $36,000 ÷ 12,000 = $3

   Allocated Cost
   Product A 8,000 x $2 = $16,000   5,000 x $3 = $15,000
   Product B 7,000 x $2 = $14,000   7,000 x $3 = $21,000

2. d   After automation, Product A uses less labour hours but causes automation associated overhead costs such as utilities to increase. Continuing to use labour hours as the allocation base will cause more of Product A's automation costs to be allocated to Product B. Accordingly, Product A will be under costed and Product B will be over costed.

3. b   The use of labour hours as the allocation base assigns an equal amount of cost to both wicker and wrought iron furniture. Since wicker furniture requires more machine set-ups and more expensive packaging it should be assigned a higher amount of overhead cost. Accordingly, wicker furniture is under costed while wrought iron furniture is over costed. As a result, wicker furniture is under priced and wrought iron furniture is overpriced. Activity based costing would improve the accuracy of the allocations and thereby result in a more reasonable pricing practice.

4. c   Since indirect material usage is directly linked to the volume of production (i.e., the more units produced the more materials used), the use of a volume based cost driver should fairly allocate indirect materials costs to products.

5. d
   Carburetors 20
   Air Filters 30
   Total 50

   Overhead Rate $22,000 ÷ 50 = $440

   Allocated Cost
   Carburetors 20 x $440 = $8,800
   Air Filters 30 x $440 = $13,200

6. a
   Carburetors 7,500
   Air Filters 12,500
   Total 20,000

   Overhead Rate $100,000 ÷ 20,000 = $5

   Allocated Cost
   Carburetors 7,500 x $5 = $37,500
   Air Filters 12,500 x $5 = $62,500

7. b Using direct labour hours as the allocation base would act to assign an equal amount of overhead cost to carburetors and air filters. If storage space is the appropriate cost driver, air filters should be assigned 2/3 (i.e., 4,000 / 6,000) of the product-level overhead cost. Therefore, the use of direct labour as an allocation base would act to under cost air filters and to over cost carburetors.

8. c

9. b

10. b Increasing voluntary quality cost would decrease failure costs leading to increased customer satisfaction and an improved quality image.

11. c Voluntary costs such as prevention and appraisal are directly controllable by increasing or decreasing the funding directed to those activities. While managers can indirectly affect failure costs by controlling voluntary costs, they cannot directly controlled those failure costs.

12. a Increases in voluntary costs such as prevention and appraisal act to decrease failure costs.

13. c

Solutions to Exercise Type Problems

P1. Solution for Requirement 1

	Before Automation	After Automation
Overhead Rate	$90,000 + 100,000 = $0.90	$220,000 + 50,000 = $4.40
Allocated Cost		
Bikes	80,000 x $0.90 = $72,000	30,000 x $4.40 = $132,000
Rowers	20,000 x $0.90 = $18,000	20,000 x $4.40 = $ 88,000

As the above computations show, the amount of overhead cost allocated to the rowing machines increased from $18,000 to $88,000. Two factors caused this dramatic increase. First, the amount of total overhead cost to be allocated increased form $90,000 to $220,000. Next, the automation acted to reduce the total labour required to make the bike machines. Accordingly, labour hours devoted to rowers moved from a proportion of 20,000 hours out of 100,000 hours to 20,000 out of 50,000. While only 20% (20,000 + 100,000) of the total cost was allocated to rowers before automation, 40% (20,000 + 50,000) of the total cost was allocated to rowers after automation.

P1. Solution for Requirement 2

	Before Automation	After Automation
Overhead Rate	$90,000 + 100,000 = $0.90	$220,000 + 44,000 = $5.00
Allocated Cost		
Bikes	80,000 x $0.90 = $72,000	40,000 x $5.00 = $200,000
Rowers	20,000 x $0.90 = $18,000	4,000 x $5.00 = $ 20,000

P1. Solution for Requirement 3

Machine hours appears to be a more rational allocation base for the assignment of utility cost. Since machinery uses electricity, the more machine hours used the higher the utility cost. Accordingly, there is a logical link between machine hours and utility cost. Note that there was a slight increase in the overhead cost allocated to rowers after automation. This may have occurred because utility costs were not accurately linked to labour hours before automation as well as after automation. While machine hours appears to be the best allocation base for utility cost, machine hours should not be used for all overhead costs. For example, fringe benefits cost are more closely linked to labour hours than to machine hours. Finn's operations may have reached the point where multiple cost drivers must be used in order to accomplish accurate allocations.

P2. Solution for Requirement 1

Since it requires the same amount of labour to make a hammer or a wrench (i.e., 15 minutes), labour hours would assign the same overhead cost per unit to hammers and wrenches. This is inappropriate because the per unit cost of batch-level, product-level, and facility-level costs is higher for wrenches than for hammers. For example, set-up costs are $1,200 per batch ($288,000 ÷ 240 set ups). Since a batch of hammers contains 100,000 units, the set up cost per unit is $0.012. Compare this with the $0.12 ($1,200 ÷ 1,000 units) cost per unit for wrenches.

P2. Solution for Requirement 2

The activity based cost data suggest that an equal amount of batch, product, and facility-level costs should be assigned to hammers and wrenches. A volume based cost driver such as labour hours assigns more overhead costs to products that are produced in greater volume. Accordingly, using direct labour hours would assign too much overhead cost to hammers and too little to wrenches. Under a cost plus pricing practice, hammers would be overpriced and wrenches would be underpriced.

P2. Solution for Requirement 3

Allocation for Hammers

Cost	Cost ÷ Driver	Allocation = Rate	Weight x of Base	Allocated Cost
$360,000	300,000	1.20	30,000*	$ 36,000
288,000	240	1200.00	12	14,400
93,000	%	0.10	$93,000	9,300
69,000	60,000	1.15	3,000	3,450
Total Allocated Cost				$63,150

*12 setups x 10,000 units = 120,000 units x 15 minutes = 1,800,000 minutes ÷ 60 minutes = 30,000 hours

Cost Per Unit for Hammers $63,150 ÷ 120,000 = $0.53

Allocation for Wrenches:

Cost	Cost ÷ Driver	Allocation = Rate	Weight x of Base	Allocated Cost
$360,000	300,000	1.20	3,000*	$3,600
288,000	240	1200.00	12	14,400
93,000	%	0.10	$93,000	9,300
69,000	60,000	1.15	3,000	3,450
Total Allocated Cost				$30,750

*12 setups x 1,000 units = 12,000 units x 15 minutes = 180,000 minutes + 60 minutes = 3,000 hours

Cost Per Unit for Wrenches $30,750 + 12,000 = $2.56

P3. Solution for Requirement

Prevention and appraisal costs have been reduced significantly between 20X2 and 20X3. It appears that the company attempted to introduce a cost cutting campaign to reduce its voluntary quality costs. Unfortunately, as the voluntary costs were decreased the failure costs increased. Since the increase in the failure costs exceeded the cost savings generated by cutting the voluntary cost, total cost increased from $1,300,000 to $1,700,000. Accordingly, the strategy to reduce total quality cost was unsuccessful.

Chapter 7
Planning for Profit and Cost Control

Learning Objectives for the Chapter

The material in this chapter of the study guide is designed to facilitate your ability to:

- Understand budgeting as a planning process.
- Identify and describe the three levels of planning for business activity.
- Understand the advantages of budgeting.
- Appreciate the human factor in the budget process.
- Identify the primary components of a master budget.
- Prepare a sales budget and associated schedule of cash receipts.
- Prepare a purchases budget and associated schedule of cash payments.
- Prepare a selling and administrative expense budget and associated schedule of cash payments.
- Prepare a cash budget.
- Prepare a set of pro forma financial statements including an income statement, balance sheet, and cash flow statement.

Brief Explanation of the Learning Objectives

Understand budgeting as a planning process.

Budgeting is a financial description of a company's plans to obtain its objectives. Plans are frequently classified depending on the span of time they cover. Short term plans describe activities that are expected to occur within one to three years. Intermediate plans cover a three to five year span of time. Long range plans involve goals that are expected to be accomplished within five to ten years. Events expected to occur beyond ten years into the future are so uncertain that most organizations do not establish formal plans for dealing with them.

Identify and describe the three levels of planning for business activity.

The following is a description of the three levels of planning that apply to business practice:

(1) **Strategic planning** involves making long-term decisions such as defining the scope of the business, determining which products to develop, deciding whether to discontinue a product, and determining which market niche would be most profitable. Upper-level management is responsible for these decisions.

(2) **Capital budgeting** deals with intermediate range planning. It involves making decisions such as whether to buy or lease equipment, to stimulate sales, or to increase the company's asset base.

(3) **Operating budgeting** involves the establishment of a master budget that will direct the firm's activities over the short term. The master budget states objectives in specific quantities and includes sales targets, production objectives, and financing plans.

Understand the advantages of budgeting.

The following is a description of the four primary advantages of budgeting:

(1) **Planning** The budget formalizes the manager's plans in a document that clearly communicates objectives to both superiors and subordinates.

(2) **Coordination** An action that is beneficial to one part of an organization may have detrimental effects for another part of the organization. Accordingly, if all managers seek to optimize their personal performance, the organization as a whole may suffer. The budgeting process forces departments to coordinate their activities to ensure the attainment of the objectives of the firm as a whole.

(3) **Performance Measurement** Budgets represent a specific, quantitative statement of management's objectives. As such, budgets represent standards that can be used to evaluate performance.

(4) **Corrective Action** Budgeting provides advance notice of shortages, bottlenecks, or other weaknesses in operating plans. As such, budgets provide an early warning system that advises managers of potential trouble spots in time for them to react in a calm and rational manner.

Appreciate the human factor in the budget process.

Many people have a natural aversion to budgeting for a variety of reasons. First, budgets often have a constraining effect. The freedom to follow an individual's own whim is certainly more appealing than the rigor of sticking to an established plan. Further, evaluation related to budgeted expectations frightens many people. It is upper-level management's responsibility to appease the concerns of their employees and to motivate acceptance of the budgeting process among their subordinates. Many managers use **participative budgeting** to accomplish this task. As its name implies, this technique encourages participation in the budget process by employees at all levels of the organization. Because they are directly responsible for accomplishing the budget objectives, subordinates are able to make more realistic estimates of what can be attained. Participation encourages subordinates to be more cooperative, less fearful, and more highly motivated. Upper management participates in the process by ensuring that the employee-generated objectives are consistent with the company's objectives. Also, involvement by upper management restricts subordinates efforts to shirk work via the establishment of lax standards.

Identify the primary components of a master budget.

The three main components of the master budget include (1) operating budgets, (2) capital budgets, (3) financial statement budgets. The **operating budgets** describe the specific plans for running the business. Some of the specific areas included in the operating budgets are a sales budget, an inventory purchases budget, a selling and administrative budget, and a cash budget. The **capital budget** describes the company's long-term plans regarding investments in facilities, equipment, new products, store outlets, and lines of business. Information in the capital budget is frequently used as input in the operating budgets. For example, the cash budget would reflect the expected purchases of equipment that appear in the capital budget. Information contained in the operating budgets is used to prepare the **financial statement budgets**. The number of financial statement budgets, also called **pro forma statements**, depends on the nature and needs of the organization. At a minimum, most companies prepare a pro forma income statement, balance sheet, and cash flow statement.

Prepare a sales budget and associated schedule of cash receipts.

The sales forecast is the starting point in the preparation of the operating budgets. The sales budget is used to prepare the schedule of cash receipts. As its name implies the schedule of cash receipts shows when the cash inflow from sales transactions is expected to be collected. The sales budget and the associated schedule of cash receipts contain information that is used to prepare the pro forma financial statements. More specifically, the ending balance of accounts receivable is drawn from the sales budget and appears on the pro forma balance sheet. The total amount of sales contained in the sales budget is shown on the income statement. Finally, the cash amount of cash collections shown in the schedule of cash receipts will appear in the cash budget.

Prepare a purchases budget and associated schedule of cash payments.

After the amount of projected sales has been established, the budgeting process focuses on the amount of inventory that will be needed to satisfy the sales demand. Meeting the sales demand requires enough inventory to cover expected sales and to provide an amount of inventory that is adequate to cover future sales between reorder points. Accordingly, *the total amount of inventory needed for each month is equal to the amount of budgeted sales plus the desired ending inventory*. The total amount of inventory needed can be obtained from two sources. First, the company can draw down on existing stock. In other words, customer demand can be satisfied with goods that are in beginning inventory. The difference between the amount of goods needed and the beginning inventory is the amount of goods to be purchased. Accordingly, the purchases budget follows a logical format that is summarized below:

Cost of Budgeted Sales	XXX
Plus Desired Ending Inventory	XXX
Inventory Needed	XXX
Less Beginning Inventory	(XXX)
Amount to Purchase	XXX

The inventory purchases budget is used to prepare the schedule of cash payments. As its name implies the schedule of cash payments shows when the cash outflow from purchases transactions is expected to be paid. The inventory purchases budget and the associated schedule of cash payments contain information that is used to prepare the pro forma financial statements. More specifically, the ending inventory balance and the balance of accounts payable are drawn from the purchases budget. Both of these items (inventory and payables) appear on the pro forma balance sheet. The total amount of cost of goods sold is drawn from the purchases budget and is shown on the income statement. Finally, the amount of cash payments for inventory shown in the schedule of cash payments will appear in the cash budget.

Prepare a selling and administrative expense budget and associated schedule of cash payments.

The expected selling and administrative expenses are shown in the selling and administrative expense budget. This budget is used to prepare the schedule of cash payments for selling and administrative expenses. The expense items contained in the selling and administrative expense budget are shown in the pro forma income statement. Accounts payable balances associated with selling and administrative expenses and the amount of additions to accumulated amortization are drawn from the selling and administrative budget and are shown on the pro forma balance sheet. Finally, the amount of cash payments for selling and administrative expenses shown in the schedule of cash payments will appear in the cash budget.

Prepare a cash budget.

The cash budget is composed of three major components including: (1) a cash receipts section, (2) a cash payments section, and (3) financing section. Most of the raw data that is needed to prepare the cash budget is included in the cash receipts and payments schedules that have been discussed previously. Data in the cash budget constitute the primary source of information for the pro forma cash flow statement. Also, the cash budget contains the amount of the ending cash balance and the balance of notes payable that will appear on the pro forma balance sheet. The amount of interest expense shown in the cash budgets appears on the pro forma income statement.

Prepare a set of pro forma financial statements including an income statement, balance sheet, and cash flow statement.

Pro forma statements have the same appearance as other financial statements. The difference is that they contain data regarding expected future events rather than historical facts. As previously indicated the data for the pro forma statements is drawn from the operating budgets and the associated schedules of cash receipts and payments.

Self-Study Problems

Multiple Choice Problems

1. The master budget is primarily concerned with:
   a. short-range decisions
   b. intermediate range decisions
   c. long-range decisions
   d. none of the above

2. Capital budgeting deals with:
   a. short-range purchase decisions
   b. intermediate to long-term asset management decisions
   c. perpetual budgeting decisions
   d. divisional variance analysis

3. Which of the following would not be included in the cash budget?
   a. cash collections from sales
   b. cash payments for selling and administrative expense
   c. cost of good sold
   d. interest expense

4. Participative budgeting involves:
   a. low-level operational employees
   b. middle management
   c. upper-level executives
   d. all of the above

5. The starting point in the preparation of the master budget is:
   a. schedule of cash receipts
   b. purchases budget
   c. sales budget
   d. schedule of cash payments for selling and administrative expense

Use the following information to answer the next two questions:
Nash Company showed the following expected total sales:

Month	Sales
May	$60,000
June	$45,000
July	$55,000
August	$50,000

The company expects 40% of its sales to be on account (credit sales). Credit sales are collected as follows: 30% in the month of sale, 65% in the month following the sale with the remainder being uncollectible and written off in the month following the sale.

6. The budgeted accounts receivable balance on July 30th is:
   a. $22,000
   b. $12,000
   c. $15,400
   d. $14,300

7. The total cash inflows from the collection of receivables in June would be:
   a. $44,400
   b. $5,400
   c. $13,500
   d. $21,000

8. The Los Alamos Company is in the process of preparing a purchases budget for the second quarter of the 20X6 year. Forecasts of sales for the second quarter follow:

April, 20X6	14,900 units
May, 20X6	13,500 units
June, 20X6	16,200 units

   The March 20X6 sales were 12,500 units. Cost of goods sold is expected to be $8 per unit. Los Alamos would like to have ending inventory each month equal to 15% of the following month's predicted sales. The total cost of purchases in April is:
   a. $117,600
   b. $108,000
   c. $119,200
   d. none of the above

Use the following information to answer the next two questions:

Purchases on account are given below:

JANUARY	FEBRUARY	MARCH
25,000	30,000	35,000

80% of the month's purchases will be paid in the month of the purchase, the remaining 20% will be paid in the following month.

9. How much will the cash payment be in February?
   a 24,000
   b. 25,000
   c. 29,000
   d. 30,000

10. How much will the cash payment be in March?
    a. 21,00
    b. 23,000
    c. 28,000
    d. 34,000

11. The accounts payable balance at the beginning of the year was $32,600. The company purchased $180,300 worth of goods on account, and the ending balance of the payables account was $28,900. Payments on account were:
    a. $184,000
    b. $196,600
    c. $207,500
    d. $241,800

12. The Carraway Company expects to begin operating on January 1. The Company's master budget contained the following selling and administrative expense budget for January.

	January
Salary Expense	20,000
Sales Commissions 5% of Sales	10,000
Utilities	1,200
Amortization on Store Equipment	2,000
Rent	2,400
Miscellaneous	600
Total Operating Expenses	36,200

    Sales commissions are paid in cash in the month following the month in which the expense is recognized. All other expense items requiring cash payment are paid in the month in which they are recognized. The amount of cash paid for operating expenses during the month of January is:
    a. $24,200
    b. $24,200
    c. $36,200
    d. none of the above

13. Sales commissions are 10% of sales. What amount of sales commissions would be transferred to the pro forma income statement for the quarter? Sales for the quarter are given as follows:

OCTOBER	NOVEMBER	DECEMBER
32,000	24,000	46,000

   a. 3,200
   b. 10,200
   c. 1,020
   d. 13,800

14. XYZ Company started the period with $35,000 cash. Cash receipts for January were expected to total $171,000. Cash disbursements for January were expected to be $158,000. What is the expected cash balance to be at the end of January?
   a. $13,000
   b. $48,000
   c. $35,000
   d. none of the above

15. Manufacturing overhead expenses for Candy Corp. are budgeted at $2,000 per month. Included in the $2,000 are $500 worth of monthly amortization expense, and $200 worth of allocated expenses related to manufacturing insurance that is paid in September. What is the cash outflow for overhead for the month of May?
   a. $ 200
   b. $ 500
   c. $1,300
   d. $1,200

16. ABC Company budgeted the following transactions for May 20X3:

Sales (60% collected in month of sale)	$180,000
Cash Operating Expenses	105,000
Cash Purchases of Capital Investments	50,000
Cash Repayment on Note Payable	40,000
Amortization on Equipment	25,000

There was a $35,000 beginning cash balance. Sales for April were $75,000 with 40% expected to be collected in the month following the sales. The company desires to have a $20,000 ending cash balance. Determine the amount of cash overage or shortage.
   a. $42,000 shortage
   b. 23,000 overage
   c. $22,000 shortage
   d. $43,000 overage

17. The Bacon Company expects credit sales for June to be $60,000. Cash sales are expected to be $10,000. The company expects credit and cash sales to increase 15% each month. Credit sales are collected in the month following the month in which sales are made. Based on this information the amount of cash collections from sales in July would be:
   a. $80,500
   b. $71,500
   c. $11,500
   d. $70,000

Exercise Type Problems

P1. The Phone Store, Inc. (PSI) plans to open a retail store on June 1. PSI expects sales on account in June to be $50,000. Cash sales for June are expected to be $10,000. The company expects a 20% growth rate for the months of July and 20% for August. PSI normally collects 50% of accounts receivable in the month of sale, 40% in the month following the month of sale and 10% in the second month following the month of sale. Remember operations begin on June 1.

Required:

1. Prepare a sales budget for June, July and August.
2. Determine the amount of sales revenue that would appear on the August 31 pro forma income statement.
3. Prepare a cash receipts schedule for June, July, and August.
4. Determine the amount of accounts receivable that would appear on the August 31 pro forma balance sheet.

P1. Form for Requirement 1

Sales Budget	June	July	August	Total
Sales on Account				
Cash Sales				
Total Sales	$60,000	$72,000	$86,400	$218,400

P1. Form for Requirement 2

P1. Form for Requirement 3

Schedule of Cash Receipts	June	July	August
Receipts from June Sales on Account			
Receipts from July Sales on Account			
Receipts from August Sales on Account			
Receipts from June Cash Sales			
Total	$35,000	$62,000	$79,400

P1. Form for Requirement 4

P2. The controller for Tape Dispensers, Inc. (TDI) prepared the following cost of goods sold budget for the months of October, November, and December.

	October	November	December
Budgeted Cost of Goods Sold	$40,000	$50,000	$80,000

The following balances existed as of October 1: Inventory -- $3,600. Accounts Payable -- $14,800. TDI desires to maintain an ending inventory balance that is equal to 10% of the current period's cost of goods sold. All purchase are made on account. TDI pays 60% of the accounts payable balance in the month of purchase and the remaining 40% in the month following the month of purchase.

Required:

1. Prepare an inventory purchases budget for October, November and December.
2. Determine the amount of ending inventory that will appear on the end-of-quarter, December 31 pro forma balance sheet.
3. Prepare a schedule of cash payments for inventory for October, November, and December.
4. Determine the balance in accounts payable that will appear on the end-of-quarter, December 31 pro forma balance sheet.

P2. Form for Requirement 1

Inventory Purchases Budget	October	November	December
Budgeted Cost of Goods Sold			
Plus Desired Ending Inventory			
Inventory Needed			
Less Beginning Inventory			
Required Purchases (on Account)	$40,400	$51,000	$83,000

P2. Form for Requirement 2

P2. Form for Requirement 3

Schedule of Cash Payments	October	November	December
Payment of Current Accounts Payable			
Payment of Previous Accounts Payable			
Total Budgeted Payments for Inventory	$39,040	$46,760	$70,200

P2. Form for Requirement 4

P3. The following cash flow data was drawn from Car Care Company's (CCC) schedules of cash receipts and payments.

	January	February	March
Cash Receipts	160,000	188,000	225,600
Cash Payments			
For Inventory Purchases	153,526	134,230	164,152
For S&A Expenses	42,800	52,560	54,432

On January 1, CCC had a cash balance of $18,000. The company desires to maintain a cash cushion of $10,000 before making a monthly interest payment. Funds are assumed to be borrowed on the first day of each month and repaid on the last day of each month. Interest is charged at the rate of 1% per month. The company had a beginning balance in its line of credit liability account of $70,000.

Required:

1. Prepare a cash budget. Round all computations to the nearest whole dollar.

2. Determine the amount of the line of credit liability that would appear on the end-of-quarter, December 31 pro forma balance sheet.

3. Determine the amount of the cash balance that would appear on the end-of-quarter, December 31 pro forma balance sheet.

4. Determine the amount of interest expense that would appear on the end-of-quarter, December 31 pro forma income statement.

P3. Form for Requirement 1

Cash Budget	January	February	March
Beginning Cash Balance			
Add Cash Receipts			
Cash Available (a)			
Less Cash Payments			
For Inventory Purchases			
For S&A Expenses			
Total Budgeted Payments (b)			
Payments Minus Receipts			
Shortage (Surplus) (b – a)			
Plus Cash Cushion			
Financing Activity			
Borrowing (Repayment) (c)			
Interest Exp at 1% per month (d)			
Ending Cash Balance (a – b + c – d)	$ 9,017	$ 9,019	$ 9,079

P3. Form for Requirement 2

P3. Form for Requirement 3

P3. Form for Requirement 4

Multiple Choice Problems - Solutions

1. a

2. b

3. c

4. d

5. c

6. c $55,000 x .4 x .7 = $15,400

7. d $60,000 x .4 x .65 = $15,600
         $45,000 x .4 x .30 =   5,400
                              $21,000

8. a   Beginning Inventory 14,900 x $8 x .15 = $17,880.
         Ending Inventory 13,500 x $8 x .15 = $16,200

Sales	$119,200
Ending Inventory	16,200
Inventory Needed	$135,400
Beginning Inventory	(17,800)
Purchases	$117,600

9. c

January $25,000 x .20	$ 5,000
February $30,000 x .80	24,000
	$29,000

10. d

February $30,000 x .20	$ 6,000
March $35,000 x .80	28,000
	$34,000

11. a   Beginning Balance + Purchases − Cash Payments = Ending Balance
          $32,600 + $180,300 − Cash Payments = $28,900
          Cash Payments = $184,000

12. a

	January
Salary Expense	$20,000
Utilities	1,200
Rent	2,400
Miscellaneous	600
Total Cash Operating Expenses	$24,200

13. b

October 32,000 x .1		3,200
November 24,000 x .1		2,400
December 46,000 x .1		4,600
Total		10,200

14. b

Receipts	$171,000
Disbursements	(158,000)
Beginning Cash Balance	35,000
Ending Cash Balance	48,000

15. c

Budgeted Expenses	$2,000
Amortization – Non Cash	(500)
Insurance Allocation – Non Cash	(200)
Cash Outflow	$1,300

16. a

Beginning Cash Balance	$ 35,000
Collections from April Sales ($75,000 x .4)	30,000
Collections from May Sales ($180,000 x .6)	108,000
Payments for Operating Expenses	(105,000)
Cash Purchase for Capital Investments	(50,000)
Cash Payment of Note Payable	(40,000)
Cash Shortage Before Cushion	(22,000)
Cash Cushion	(20,000)
Total Cash Shortage	$(42,000)

17. b

Collections from June Sales	$60,000
Cash Sales for July ($10,000 x 1.15)	11,500
Total Cash Shortage	$71,500

Exercise Type Problems - Solutions

P1. Solution for Requirement 1

Sales Budget	June	July	August	Total
Sales on Account	$50,000	$60,000	$72,000	$182,000
Cash Sales	10,000	12,000	14,400	$36,400
Total Sales	$60,000	$72,000	$86,400	$218,400

P1. Solution for Requirement 2

Sales revenue for the quarter is equal to the sum of the monthly amounts (i.e., $60,000 + $72,000 + $86,400 = $218,400).

P1. Solution for Requirement 3

Schedule of Cash Receipts	June	July	August

Receipts from June Sales on Account	$25,000	$20,000	$5,000
Receipts from July Sales on Account		30,000	24,000
Receipts from August Sales on Account			36,000
Receipts from June Cash Sales	10,000	12,000	14,400
Total	$35,000	$62,000	$79,400

P1. Solution for Requirement 4

The accounts receivable as of August 31, 20X6 is equal to the amount due to be collected in April and May (i.e., [.1 x 60,000] + [.5 x 72,000] = $42,000).

P2. Solution for Requirement 1

Inventory Purchases Budget	October	November	December
Budgeted Cost of Goods Sold	$40,000	$50,000	$80,000
Plus Desired Ending Inventory	4,000	5,000	8,000
Inventory Needed	44,000	55,000	88,000
Less Beginning Inventory	3,600	4,000	5,000
Required Purchases (on Account)	$40,400	$51,000	$83,000

P2. Solution for Requirement 2

Since the quarter ends on December 30, the ending inventory for December is also the ending inventory for the quarter (i.e., $8,000).

P2. Solution for Requirement 3

Schedule of Cash Payments	October	November	December
Payment of Current Accounts Payable	$24,240	$30,600	$49,800
Payment of Previous Accounts Payable	14,800	16,160	20,400
Total Budgeted Payments for Inventory	$39,040	$46,760	$70,200

P2. Solution for Requirement 4

Since 60% of the current purchases on account are paid in cash during the month of purchase, 40% will remain payable at the end of the month (i.e., $83,000 x .40 = $33,200).

P3. Solution for Requirement 1

Cash Budget	January	February	March
Beginning Cash Balance	$ 18,000	$ 9,017	$ 9,019
Add Cash Receipts	160,000	188,000	225,600
Cash Available (a)	178,000	197,017	234,619
Less Cash Payments			
For Inventory Purchases	153,526	134,230	164,152
For S&A Expenses	42,800	52,560	54,432
Total Budgeted Payments (b)	196,326	186,790	218,584
Payments Minus Receipts			
Shortage (Surplus) (b – a)	18,326	(10,227)	(16,035)
Plus Cash Cushion	10,000	10,000	10,000
Financing Activity			
Borrowing (Repayment) (c)	28,326	(227)	(6,035)
Interest Exp at 1% per month (d)	(983)[1]	(981)[2]	(921)[3]
Ending Cash Balance (a – b + c – d)	$ 9,017	$ 9,019	$ 9,089

[1] ($70,000 + $28,326) X 1% = $984 (rounded)
[2] ($70,000 + $28,326 – $227) X 1% = $983 (rounded)
[3] (($70,000 + $28,326 – $227 – $6,035) X 1% = $921 (rounded)

P3. Solution for Requirement 2

$70,000 + $28,326 – $227 – $6,035 = $92,064

P3. Solution for Requirement 3

$9,089 For computations see ending cash balance in the cash budget shown in Requirement 1 above.

P3. Solution for Requirement 4

The interest expense is the total amount of the interest expense for January, February, March shown in the cash budget in Requirement 1 (i.e., $983 + $981 + $921 = $2,885).

Chapter 8
Performance Evaluation

Learning Objectives for the Chapter

The material in this chapter of the study guide is designed to facilitate your ability to:

- Distinguish between flexible and static budgets.
- Understand how spreadsheet software can be used to prepare flexible budgets.
- Compute revenue and cost variances and to interpret those variances as indicative of favourable or unfavourable performance.
- Compute sales activity variances (differences between static and flexible budgets), and explain how the volume variance affects fixed versus variable costs.
- Compute and interpret flexible budget variances (differences between a flexible budget and actual results) (i.e., differences between a flexible budget and actual results).
- Appreciate the human response to flexible budget variances.
- Appreciate the process of setting standards.
- Understand the criteria for selecting the variances that are most appropriate for investigation.
- Calculate price and usage variances.
- Identify the responsible parties for price and usage variances.
- Understand the basic procedures for recording variances in a general ledger.

Brief Explanation of the Learning Objectives

Distinguish between flexible and static budgets.

Recall from Chapter 7 that a master budget is based solely on the level of planned activity. Due to its rigid dependency on a single estimate of volume, the master budget is frequently called a **static budget**. In other words, the master budget remains static (i.e., stays the same) when the volume of activity changes. **Flexible budgets** differ from static budgets in that they show the estimated amount of revenues and costs that are expected at a variety of different levels of activity.

Understand how spreadsheet software can be used to prepare flexible budgets.

The computational power of spreadsheet software, such as Excel, can be used to prepare flexible budgets with very little human effort. Formulas that reference input cells are used to compute the amounts of revenue and cost shown in the budget. When the data in the input cell is changed, the software program automatically revises the amounts in the budget. For example, the spreadsheet cells containing the amount of budget revenue and cost may contain formulas that multiply the per unit sales price and cost times a referenced input cell that contains the sales volume. When the amount of sales volume in the input cell is changed, all amounts in the entire budget are recomputed automatically.

Compute revenue and cost variances and interpret those variances as indicative of favourable or unfavourable performance

One means of evaluating managerial performance is to compare standard amounts with the actual results. The differences between the standard and actual amounts are called **variances**. Variances can be either favourable or unfavourable. Since managers seek to maximize revenue, a **favourable sales variance** occurs when actual sales revenue is greater than expected (i.e., standard) sales. An **unfavourable sales variance** occurs when actual sales are less than expected. Since managers try to minimize costs, **favourable cost variances** occur when actual costs are below standard costs. **Unfavourable cost variances** occur when actual costs are greater than standard costs. These relationships are summarized below.

```
When Actual Sales are   >   Expected Sales, Variances are Favourable
When Actual Sales are   <   Expected Sales, Variances are Unfavourable
When Actual Costs are   >   Standard Costs, Variances are Unfavourable
When Actual Costs are   <   Standard Costs, Variances are Favourable
```


Compute sales activity variances (differences between static and flexible budgets), and explain how the volume variance affects fixed versus variable costs.

The amount of a sales activity variance is determined by the difference between the static budget which is based on the planned volume and a flexible budget prepared at the actual volume. This variance provides a measure of how effective managers are at attaining the planned volume of activity. Total fixed costs will remain the same regardless of the volume of activity. Total variable costs will increase or decrease in direct proportion with the volume of production. Since the volume of production is controlled by level of sales activity, marketing managers are normally held accountable for the volume variances.

Compute and interpret flexible budget variances (differences between a flexible budget and actual results).

For purposes of performance evaluation, a flexible budget prepared at the actual volume of activity is compared to actual results. Since the volume of activity is the same for the flexible budget and the actual results, any reported variances are caused by differences between the standard and actual per unit amounts. The flexible budget cost variances provide insight into how efficiently managers have operated the business. For example, a favourable materials variance may indicate that managers were shrewd in negotiating price concessions, discounts, or delivery terms that reduced the price paid for materials. Similarly, managers may have used materials efficiently thereby reducing the quantity of material used. In contrast, the unfavourable labour variance may indicate that managers have been lax in controlling the wages paid to employees or failed to motivate their employees to work hard. Flexible budget cost variances must be analyzed carefully. A variance that appears to be favourable on the surface may, in fact, be unfavourable. For example, a favourable materials variance may have been obtained by paying low prices for inferior goods. The substandard materials may have required additional labour in the production process, which would cause an unfavourable labour variance. Variances do not imply positive or negative performance. They merely signal the need for investigation.

Appreciate the human response to flexible budget variances.

In general, variances should not be used to single out managers for praise or punishment. The purpose of variances is to provide information that facilitates efficiency and improves productivity. If they are misused as a means of dolling out rewards and punishment, managers are likely to respond by withholding or manipulating information. For example, a manager may manipulate the determination of the standard cost by deliberately overstating the amount of materials and/or labour that is expected to be required to complete a job. Later, the manager's performance will be evaluated as good when the actual cost of materials and/or labour is lower than the inflated standard. Indeed, this practice has become so common that it has been given a name. The difference between inflated and realistic standards is called **budget slack**. A similar game played with respect to revenue is called **lowballing**. In this case, the sales staff deliberately underestimates the amount of expected sales. Later when actual sales exceed expected sales, sales personnel are rewarded for exceeding the budget. If standards are used solely for punitive purposes, gamesmanship will rapidly degrade the standard costing system.

Appreciate the process of setting standards.

Establishing standards is probably the most difficult task required in the development of a standard cost system. The standards represent what should be based on a certain set of anticipated circumstances. *Historical data* provides a good starting point for the establishing standards. This data must be updated for changes in technology, in plant layout, in new methods of production, in worker productivity, etc. *Behavioural implications* must also be considered when developing standards. Finally, management should also consider the desired level of difficulty necessary to achieve standard performance. The ranges of difficulty can be subdivided into three logical alternatives: (1) Ideal Standards, (2) Practical Standards, and (3) Lax Standards.

- **Ideal standards** represent perfection. They show what costs should be under ideal circumstances. They ignore allowances for normal materials waste and spoilage. They do not consider ordinary labour inefficiencies due to machine down time, cleanup, breaks, or personal needs. Ideal standards are beyond the capabilities of most, if not all, employees. Such standards may motivate some individuals to constantly strive for improvement. However, unattainable standards tend to discourage the majority of people.

- **Practical standards** can be accomplished with a reasonable degree of effort. They constitute attainable goals for employees. They allow for normal levels of inefficiency in materials and labour usage. An average worker performing in a diligent manner would be able to achieve standard performance. Practical standards have motivational appeal for most employees. The feeling of accomplishment that has been attained through earnest effort tends to encourage workers to do their best.

- **Lax standards** represent easily attainable goals. Standard performance can be accomplished with minimal effort. Lax standards lack motivational appeal for most people. Constant success attained with minimal effort tends to create boredom and low performance. Also, variances lose meaningful content. Deviations caused by superior or inferior performance are obscured by the built-in slack.

Understand the criteria for selecting the variances that are most appropriate for investigation.

Judgment, based on experience, plays a significant role in deciding which variances merit investigation. However, several factors that influence the decision can be identified. These include **materiality, frequency, capacity to control**, and the **characteristics of the item being considered**.

- **Materiality** Standard costs are by nature estimated figures. They cannot be perfect predictors of actual costs. Slight variances will emerge in the normal course of business. These slight variances should not be investigated because they are not likely to produce useful information.

- The **concept of frequency** of occurrence is closely related to the materiality concept. An immaterial variance that amounts to $20,000 during one month can become a material variance amounting to $240,000 if the monthly performance is repeated throughout the year. Variance reports should highlight frequent as well as large variations.

- The **capacity to control** refers to management's ability to take corrective action. If utility rates cause variances between actual and standard overhead cost, management would have little control over the variance. Conversely, if actual labour costs exceed standard costs because a supervisor is unable to motivate his employees, this would be classified as a controllable variance. Managers should concentrate on controllable variances in order to maximize their utility to the firm.

- Certain items have **characteristics that permit management abuse**. For example, managers can reduce actual costs, in the short run, by delaying expenditures for maintenance, research and development, advertising, etc. While cost reductions in these areas may produce favourable variances and immediate gratification, they will have a long-term detrimental impact on profitability. Unfortunately, managers under stress may yield to the temptations of the short-term benefits. As a result, variances associated with these critical items should be closely scrutinized.

Calculate price and usage variances.

The resources used in the manufacturing process are frequently called *inputs*. The purpose of the manufacturing process is to transform the set of **inputs** (i.e., materials, labour, and overhead) into **outputs** (i.e., products). As previously indicated, managers establish standards to exercise control over the consumption of the inputs. A **standard** represents the amount of input that management *expects* to be consumed in the manufacturing process. The *cost per unit* of an input is composed of two factors. One factor is price; the other is usage. A favourable **price variance** occurs when you pay less than you expected (i.e., standard price) to pay. An unfavourable price variance occurs when you pay more than expected. Likewise, favourable and unfavourable **usage variances** occur when you consume more or less than the standard quantity of an input. Price and usage variances are computed for each input factor in the production process including materials, labour, and variable overhead. The algebraic formula for calculating price and usage variances is shown below.

- Price Variance = |Actual Price − Standard Price| x Actual Quantity
- Usage Variance = |Actual Quantity − Standard Quantity| x Standard Price

Identify the responsible parties for price and usage variances.

The parties responsible for variances depends on many different circumstances. Consider the assumption that the purchasing agent is responsible for the price variance but has no control over the quantity used in production. While this assumption may seem logical, it may not happen this way in practice. For example, the raw materials purchasing agent can cause a quantity variance by purchasing inferior quality materials thereby leading to excess waste. Establishing responsibility requires careful investigation of the signals provided by variance analysis.

Understand the basic procedures for recording variances in a general ledger.

The recording procedures for variances are summarized on page 292 of the text.

Self-Study Problems

Multiple Choice Problems

1. A static budget...
   a. is related to the electrical budget.
   b. remains constant, regardless of actual volume of production.
   c. is adjusted for actual activity levels.
   d. is updated on a monthly basis.

2. Select the answer that is true.
   a. When Actual Sales are > Expected Sales, Variances are Unfavourable.
   b. When Actual Sales are < Expected Sales, Variances are Favourable.
   c. When Actual Costs are > Standard Costs, Variances are Favourable.
   d. Answers a, b, and c are false.

3. If actual volume is greater than expected:
   a. fixed overhead cost per unit will be higher than expected
   b. fixed overhead cost per unit will be lower than expect
   c. variable cost per unit will not be affected
   d. b and c

4. Lowballing occurs when:
   a. marketing managers deliberately underestimate expected sales
   b. production managers deliberately overestimate expected material usage
   c. sales personnel deliberately overestimate expected sales
   d. personnel managers deliberately underestimate expected labour rates

5. Which of the following represents the type of standards that are most likely to motivate employees to maximize their performance?
   a. ideal standards
   b. practical standards
   c. lax standards
   d. All three choices are likely to have the same effect on employee motivation.

Use the following information to answer the next two questions: The following master budget was drawn from the records of AXE Company. The master budget was based on a planned volume of activity of 5,000 units:

Revenues	$50,000
Variable Cost	(35,000)
Contribution Margin	15,000
Fixed Costs	(5,000)
Net Income	$10,000

6. If AXE actually produces 6,000 units, the flexible budget would show total **variable cost** of:
   a. $15,000
   b. $35,000
   c. $42,000
   d. $6,00

7. If AXE actually produced 4,500 units, the flexible budget would show fixed costs amounting to:
   a. $4,500
   b. $1.00 per unit
   c. $5,000
   d. a and b

Use the following information to answer the next four questions: Cole Manufacturing Company expects its variable cost per unit to be $25. Fixed costs are expected to be $69,000. Cole plans to make and sell 5,000 units of product. The expected sales price is $45 per unit. Each of the following four multiple choice questions should be considered independently. In other words, the facts described in one question should be ignored when considering the other questions.

8. Assume that Cole reduces the actual sales price to $43 in order to increase actual sales to 5,300 units. The implementation of this strategy will:
   a. produce a favourable sales volume variance of $13,500
   b. produce an unfavourable sales price variance of $10,600
   c. produce a favourable total sales variance of $2,900
   d. all of the above

9. Assume that actual volume is 4,800 units and that the actual sales price is $47. Based on this information:
   a. the sales pricevariance would be $9,600 favourable
   b. the sales volume variance would be $9,600 unfavourable
   c. the sales volume variance would be $9,000 favourable
   d. the sales price variance would be $9,000 favourable

10. Assume that actual volume is 4,900 units and the actual variable cost per unit is $24. Based on this information:
    a. the variable cost volume variance is $2,500 favourable
    b. the variable cost flexible budget variance is $2,500 unfavourable
    c. the variable cost volume variance is $2,500 unfavourable
    d. the variable cost flexible budget variance is $2,500 favourable

11. Assume that actual volume is 4,700 units and the actual fixed cost are $72,000. Based on this information the amount of fixed cost shown in the flexible budget would be:
    a. $72,000
    b. $69,000
    c. $3,000
    d. none of the above

12. Which of the following would be responsible for generating variable cost volume variances?
    a. Purchasing agents
    b. Production managers
    c. Sales managers
    d. The company president

13. If planned activity is understated, what consequence is likely?
    a. The predetermined overhead rate will be overstated
    b. Products are underpriced
    c. Per unit fixed cost will not be affected
    d. Per unit variable overhead costs are understated

14. The Bed Company (BC) pays it production workers standard wage rate of $8 per hour to make beds. The standard amount of time required to make one bed is 3 hours. In the month of August, BC produced 190 beds. Actual labour usage amounted to 600 hours. The actual labour wage rate amounted to $8.10. Based on this information the labour price variance is:
    a. $60 unfavourable
    b. $57 favourable
    c. $60 favourable
    d. $57 unfavourable

The following information applies to the next two questions: ABC Company planned to make 50,000 units of product. SBC actually produced 51,000 units of product. The fixed cost predetermined overhead rate was $4.50 per unit. Actual fixed overhead costs amounted to $210,000.

15. The fixed cost volume variance for ABC Company is:
    a. $19,500 unfavourable
    b. $19,500 favourable
    c. $4,500 unfavourable
    d. $4,500 favourable

16. The fixed cost spending variance for ABC Company is:
    a. $15,000 unfavourable
    b. $15,000 favourable
    c. $19,500 unfavourable
    d. $19,500 unfavourable

Exercise Type Problems

P1. Hamner Manufacturing Company makes glass apples that are sold to colleges and universities. The schools use the apples as mementos to recognize excellence in teaching awards. Hamner's standard selling price of each apple is $10. The standard materials cost (i.e., variable cost) of each apple is $4. All manufacturing employees are paid on an annual salary basis. Fixed manufacturing cost including production workers salaries amount to $4,620. Fixed selling and administrative costs are expected to amount to $1,600. Hamner planed to make and sell 2,200 apples. Actual production and sales amounted to 2,400 units. The actual sales price was $9.60 per apple and the actual variable cost was $4.14 per unit. Actual fixed manufacturing cost was $3,800 and actual fixed selling and administrative cost amounted to $1,700.

Required:
1. Prepare a pro forma income statement as would appear in a master budget.
2. Prepare a pro forma income statement as would appear in a flexible budget.
3. Determine the amount of the activity (volume) variances and indicate whether the variances are favourable or unfavourable.
4. Determine the amount of the flexible budget variances and indicate whether the variances are favourable or unfavourable.

P1. Form for Requirements 1, 2, and 3.

	Master Budget 2,200 Units	Flexible Budget 2,400 Units	Activity Variances
Sales			
Variable Materials Cost			
Contribution Margin			
Fixed Manufacturing			
Fixed Selling and Admin.			
Net Income	$ 6,980	$ 8,180	1,200 F

P1. Form for Requirement 4

	Flexible Budget 2,400 Units	Actual Results 2,400 Units	Activity Variances
Sales			
Variable Materials Cost			
Contribution Margin			
Fixed Manufacturing			
Fixed Selling and Admin.			
Net Income	$ 8,180	$ 7,604	576 U

P2. This problem is an extension of Problem 1. Assume that Hamner desires to investigate the materials cost variance further. The $4 per unit of standard materials cost consisted of 2 kilograms of glass that was expected to cost $2.00 per kilogram. The actual cost of $4.14 per apple resulted from the fact that actual usage amounted 2.3 kilograms of glass per apple. The actual cost of the glass used amounted to $1.80 per kilogram.

1. Determine the amount of the price and usage variances and indicate whether the variances are favourable or unfavourable.
2. Identify the parties that are normally held accountable for the materials price variance and for the materials usage variance. Provide a logical explanation as to who was responsible for the materials cost variance in this case.
3. Based on a predetermined overhead rate of $2.10 per unit (i.e., $4,620 ÷ 2,200 units = $2.10), determine the amount of the manufacturing fixed cost spending variance and the manufacturing fixed cost volume variance and indicate whether the variances are favourable or unfavourable.

P2. Form for Requirement 1.

$$\text{Materials Price Variance} = |\text{Actual Price} - \text{Standard Price}| \times \text{Actual Quantity}$$

$$\text{Materials Usage Variance} = |\text{Actual Quantity} - \text{Standard Quantity}| \times \text{Standard Price}$$

P2. Form for Requirement 2.

P2. Form for Requirement 3.

$$\text{Fixed Overhead Volume Variance} = |\text{Applied Fixed Overhead Costs} - \text{Budgeted Fixed Overhead Costs}|$$

$$\text{Fixed Overhead Spending Variance} = |\text{Actual Fixed Overhead Costs} - \text{Budgeted Fixed Overhead Costs}|$$

Multiple Choice Problems - Solutions

1. b

2. d

3. d

4. a

5. b

6. c   Per Unit Variable Cost = $35,000 + 5,000 Units = $7 Per Unit
Total Variable Cost = 6,000 Units x $7 Per Unit = $42,000

7. c   Total fixed cost remain constant at $5,000 regardless of the level of production. Fixed cost per unit will decline as level of production increases.

8. d

	Static Budget	Flexible Budget	Actual Results
Sales Volume (a)	5,000 Units	5,300 Units	5,300 Units
Sales Price (b)	$45	$45	$43
Total Sales (a x b)	$225,000	$238,500	$227,900

Sales Volume Variance $225,000 – $238,500 = $13,500 Favourable*
    *The sales volume variance is favourable because actual units sold is more than expected sales.

Sales Price Variance $238,500 – $227,900 = $10,600 Unfavourable*
    *The sales price variance is unfavourable because the actual sales price is less than expected sales price.

Total Sales Variance $225,000 – $227,900 = $2,900 Favourable*
    *The total sales variance is favourable because the total actual sales price is more than expected sales.

9. a

	Static Budget	Flexible Budget	Actual Results
Sales Volume (a)	5,000 Units	4,800 Units	4,800 Units
Sales Price (b)	$45	$45	$47
Total Sales (a x b)	$225,000	$216,000	$225,600

Sales Volume Variance $225,000 – $216,000 = $9,000 Unfavourable*
    *The sales volume variance is favourable because actual units sold is less than expected sales.

Sales Price Variance $216,000 – $225,600 = $9,600 Favourable*
    *The sales price variance is unfavourable because the actual sales price is more than expected sales price.

10. a

	Static Budget	Flexible Budget	Actual Results
Production Volume (a)	5,000 Units	4,900 Units	4,900 Units
Variable Cost (b)	$25	$25	$24
Total Variable Cost (a x b)	$125,000	$122,500	$117,600

Variable Cost Volume Variance $125,000 − $122,500 = $2,500 Favourable*

*The variable cost volume variance is favourable because total variable cost is less than expected variable cost.

Variable Cost Flexible Budget Variance $122,500 − $117,600 = $4,900 Favourable*

*The variable cost flexible budget variance is favourable because actual total variable cost is less than the budgeted cost shown in the flexible budget.

11. b   Total budgeted fixed cost remain the same at $69,000 regardless of the volume of production.

12. c   Variable cost volume variances are caused by differences between the actual and estimated sales volume. Since marketing managers are primarily responsible for sales volume, this management group is primarily responsible for the variable cost volume variances.

13. a   The predetermined overhead rate is calculated by dividing the total expected cost by the planned volume of activity. If the planned activity is understated the denominator will be smaller than it should be thereby making the resultant rate higher than it should be (i.e., the rate is overstated).

14. c   Labour Price Variance = |Actual Price − Standard Price| x Actual Quantity
Labour Price Variance = |$8.10 − $8.00| x 600 = $60 Unfavourable*
*The variance is unfavourable because the actual labour rate is greater than the expected rate.

15. d   Fixed Overhead Volume Variance = |Applied Fixed Overhead Costs − Budgeted Fixed Overhead Costs|
Fixed Overhead Volume Variance = |(51,000 x $4.50) − (50,000 x $4.50)| = $4,500 Favourable*
*The variance is favourable because the company actually produced more units than expected, thereby reducing fixed cost per unit.

16. b   Fixed Overhead Spending Variance = |Actual Fixed Overhead Costs − Budgeted Fixed Overhead Costs|
Fixed Overhead Spending Variance = |$210,000 − (50,000 x $4.50)| = $15,000 Favourable*
*The variance is favourable because the company actually spent less for fixed cost than it expected to spend.

Exercise Type Problems - Solutions

P1. Solution for Requirements 1, 2, and 3.

	Master Budget 2,200 Units	Flexible Budget 2,400 Units	Activity Variances
Sales	$22,000 (1)	$24,000 (2)	$2,000 F
Variable Materials Cost	(8,800) (3)	(9,600) (4)	800 U
Contribution Margin	13,200	14,400	1,200 F
Fixed Manufacturing	(4,620)	(4,620)	0
Fixed Selling and Admin.	(1,600)	(1,600)	0
Net Income	$ 6,980	$ 8,180	1,200 F

(1) $10 x 2,200 Units
(2) $10 x 2,400 Units
(3) $4 x 2,200 Units
(4) $4 x 2,400 Units

P1. Solution for Requirement 4

	Flexible Budget 2,400 Units	Actual Results 2,400 Units	Activity Variances
Sales	$24,000 (1)	$23,040 (2)	$960 U
Variable Materials Cost	(9,600) (3)	(9,936) (4)	336 U
Contribution Margin	14,400	13,104	1,296 U
Fixed Manufacturing	(4,620)	(3,800)	820 F
Fixed Selling and Admin.	(1,600)	(1,700)	100 U
Net Income	$ 8,180	$ 7,604	576 U

(1) $10 x 2,400 Units
(2) $9.60 x 2,400 Units
(3) $4 x 2,400 Units
(4) $4.14 x 2,400 Units

P2. Solution for Requirement 1.

Materials Price Variance = |Actual Price − Standard Price| x Actual Quantity
Materials Price Variance = |$1.80 − $2.00| x (2.3 x 2,400) = $1,104 Favourable*
*The variance is favourable because the actual price is less than the standard price.

Materials Usage Variance = |Actual Quantity − Standard Quantity| x Standard Price
Materials Usage Variance = |(2.3 x 2,400) − (2.0 x 2,400)| x $2.00 = $1,440 Unfavourable*
*The variance is unfavourable because the actual quantity (usage) is greater than the expected usage.

P2. Solution for Requirement 2.

The purchasing agent is normally held accountable for the price variance and the production manager is held accountable for the usage variance. In this case, the purchasing agent may be due congratulations for obtaining a favourable price and the production manager may have been derelict in managing the usage of raw materials. However, it could be the case that the purchasing agent was able to obtain a reduced price by accepting low quality glass which lead to waste in the manufacturing process. In this case, corrective action should be taken to assure that, in the future, the purchasing agent buys material that meets quality standards.

P2. Solution for Requirement 3.

Fixed Overhead Volume Variance = | Applied Fixed Overhead Costs − Budgeted Fixed Overhead Costs |
Fixed Overhead Volume Variance = | (2,400 x $2.10) − (2,200 x $2.10) | = $420 Favourable*
*The variance is favourable because the company actually produced more units than expected, thereby reducing fixed cost per unit.

Fixed Overhead Spending Variance = | Actual Fixed Overhead Costs − Budgeted Fixed Overhead Costs |
Fixed Overhead Spending Variance = | $3,800 − (2,200 x $2.10) | = $820 Favourable*
*The variance is favourable because the company actually spent less for fixed cost than it expected to spend.

Chapter 9
Responsibility Accounting

Learning Objectives for the Chapter

The material in this chapter of the study guide is designed to facilitate your ability to:

- Understand the concept of decentralization and describe its relationship to responsibility accounting.
- Prepare and use responsibility reports.
- Understand the controllability concept.
- Explain how the management by exception doctrine relates to responsibility reports.
- Understand the differences in cost, profit, and investment centers.
- Evaluate investment opportunities by using the return on investment technique.
- Evaluate investment opportunities by using the residual income technique.
- Understand the three common approaches used to establish transfer prices.

Brief Explanation of the Learning Objectives

Understand the concept of decentralization and describe its relationship to responsibility accounting.

The practice of delegating authority and responsibility is referred to as decentralization. Some of the advantages of decentralization are included in the following list.

1. *Encourages upper level management to concentrate on strategic decisions.* Since local management makes the routine decisions, upper management has more time to concentrate its effort on long range planning, goal setting, and performance evaluation.
2. *Promotes improvements in decision making.* Local managers are usually better-informed about local issues. Further, their close proximity to the local issues permits them to react more rapidly to developing events. As a result, local managers are generally able to make better decisions.
3. *Motivates managers to improve productivity.* The freedom to act coupled with responsibility accounting for the actions taken results in an environment that encourages most individuals to perform at high levels.
4. *Trains lower level managers to accept higher responsibilities.* Decision-making is a general skill. Managers who are accustomed to making decisions regarding local issues are generally able to apply their decision-making skills to broader issues when they are promoted to upper management positions.

5. *Improves performance evaluation.* When lines of authority and responsibility are clearly drawn, then credit or blame can be more easily assigned to the results achieved.

Responsibility accounting focuses reporting on individual managers. For example, expense items that are controllable by the production manager are presented in a separate report from similar items that are under the control of the manager of the marketing department. The objective of responsibility accounting is to increase productivity by providing information that is helpful in evaluating managerial performance.

Prepare and use responsibility reports.

A responsibility report is prepared for each individual who has control over revenue or expense items. It normally includes a list of all the items under that person's control, the budgeted amount for each item, the actual amount for each item and the difference between the budgeted and actual amounts (i.e., the variance). The report shows the manager what was expected of him or her and how his or her actual performance compared to those expectations.

Understand the controllability concept.

The concept of control is crucial to an effective responsibility accounting system. Each manager should be evaluated on only the revenue or cost items that are under his or her control. Motivation is lost when managers are rewarded or punished for actions that are beyond the scope of their control.

Explain how the management by exception doctrine relates to responsibility reports.

Responsibility reports are arranged in a manner that promotes the use of the "management by exception doctrine." More specifically, each manager receives only summary information regarding the performance of the responsibility centers that are under his or her supervision. For example, consider a case where the manager of an assembly department reports to a production manager. The production manager will be advised as to the amount of the total budget variance incurred by the assembly department. He or she is not informed as to the cause of the variance. That information is reported only to the supervisor of the assembly department. At first glance, the lack of detailed information may appear to hinder the ability of the manager of production to control costs. In fact, it has the opposite effect. Be aware that managers are normally very busy individuals who must ration their time carefully. The supervisor of the assembly department should look at his or her responsibility report and take the necessary corrective action without bothering the production manager. The production manager should become concerned only when one of his or her supervisors loses control. The summary data in the production manager's report will be sufficient to advise him or her of such situations. Accordingly, managers will be concentrating only on the exceptional items (i.e., management by exception) which will be automatically highlighted in their responsibility reports.

Understand the differences in cost, profit, and investment centers.

A **responsibility center** is the point in an organization where the control over revenue or expense items is located. The point of control may be a division, a department, a subdepartment or even a single machine. There are three commonly recognized responsibility centers including:
1. A **cost center** is a business segment that incurs expenses but does not generate revenue.
2. A **profit center** differs from a cost center in that it not only incurs costs but also generates income.
3. **Investment center** managers are responsible for revenue and expense items and for the investment of capital.

Evaluate investment opportunities by using the return on investment technique.

Businesses use assets to obtain a greater quantity of other assets. For example, a grocery store uses cash in order to purchase inventory. Performance can be measured by the ability to increase the ratio of the assets returned to the amount of assets used. This measure is commonly referred to as the **return on investment** (ROI). The higher the ratio, the better the performance is considered to be: ROI can be expressed in a simple equation as follows:

$$ROI = \frac{Net\ Income}{Investment}$$

The return on investment formula can be subdivided into two ratios. Profitability is affected by the margin earned on sales and by the number of times that the margin is collected during the accounting period (i.e., the turnover rate). For example, an item that can be purchased for $1 and sold for $1.20 may be more profitable than an item that is purchased for $1 and sold for $1.50. If during the accounting period 75 units of the item with the 20¢ margin could be sold but only 25 units of the item with the 50¢ margin could be sold. Under these circumstances, the first item would produce $15 (i.e., 75 × $.20) of profit during the accounting period, while the second item would produce only $12.50 (i.e., 25 × $.50) of profit. Clearly, both margin and turnover affect profitability. If we express both of the factors as separate ratios, the following expanded version of the ROI formula can be developed.

$$\text{Step 1:} \quad \text{Margin} = \frac{\text{Net Income}}{\text{Sales}}$$

$$\text{Step 2: Turnover} = \frac{\text{Sales}}{\text{Investment}}$$

$$\text{Step 3:} \quad \text{ROI} = \text{Margin} \times \text{Turnover}$$

$$\text{Step 4:} \quad \text{ROI} = \frac{\text{Net Income}}{\text{Sales}} \times \frac{\text{Sales}}{\text{Investment}}$$

Evaluate investment opportunities by using the residual income technique.

A manager of an investment center may have an ROI that is higher than the company wide ROI. Suppose the manager is faced with an investment opportunity that has an ROI that is below her center's ROI but is above the company wide ROI. While the opportunity would raise the company ROI, it would decrease her center's ROI, thereby reducing her personal performance evaluation. When faced with decisions such as these, many managers will choose to benefit themselves at the expense of their corporations. The term used to describe this situation is suboptomization. In order to avoid suboptomization, many businesses use an evaluation technique known as the **residual income approach**. This approach evaluates a manager on his or her ability to maximize the dollar value of earnings above some targeted level of earnings. The targeted level of earnings is established by multiplying the amount of investment by a desired (company-wide) ROI. Expressed as a formula, residual income is defined as:

$$\text{Residual Income} = \text{Earned Income} - (\text{Investment} \times \text{Desired ROI})$$

Understand the three common approaches used to establish transfer prices.

When goods are transferred internally, the sales price of one division becomes a cost to the other division. Accordingly, the amount of profit included in the transfer price will increase the earnings of the selling division and decrease the earnings (via increased expenses) of the purchasing division. It is to the advantage of the selling division to obtain the highest price, while the purchasing division seeks the lowest price possible. When a competitive evaluation system based on profitability measures is imposed upon this situation, it is easy to understand why the **transfer price** is subject to considerable controversy. There are three common approaches used to establish transfer prices. These include:

1. **Price based on market forces.** The preferred method is to base transfer prices on some form of competitive market price. Ideally, the selling division should have the authority to sell its merchandise to outsiders as well as, or in preference to, its sister divisions. Likewise, the purchasing divisions should have the option to buy goods from outsiders if they are able to obtain favourable prices. However, both selling and purchasing divisions would be motivated to deal with each other because of savings

in selling, administrative and transportation costs that arise as a natural result of internal transactions.

2. **Price based on negotiation.** Unfortunately, in many instances market prices are not available or are not in the best interest of the company as a whole. Sometimes a division makes a unique product that is used only by one of its sister divisions. When this occurs, there is no external market to use as a deciding force in determining the transfer price. At other times, market based transfer prices may lead to suboptomization. In situations such as those described above, it is advantageous to seek a **negotiated transfer price**. When the managers involved agree to a negotiated price, the concept of fairness is preserved. Further, the element of profit remains intact; and the evaluation concepts that have been discussed in this chapter can be applied. While negotiated prices are not as good as market prices, they are able to offer many of the same advantages. Accordingly, they should act as the first possible alternate when a company is unable to use market based transfer prices.

3. **Price based on cost.** The least desirable transfer price strategy is one that is based on cost. When cost is used, you must first determine the amount of cost. Using cost as the basis for transfer prices acts to remove the profit motive. Without profitability as a guide, the incentive to control cost is diminished. Despite this potential detrimental effect, many companies continue to use cost as the basis for transfer prices because cost represents an objective number that is easy to compute.

Self-Study Problems

Multiple Choice Problems

1. Which of the following choices is considered an advantage of decentralization?
    a. Decentralization improves performance evaluation
    b. Decentralization guarantees promotions of top managers
    c. Decentralization eliminates competition between managers
    d. All of the above are advantages of decentralization

2. A manager of an investment center is responsible for:
    a. expenses, revenue, and major asset purchases
    b. only for controlling expenses
    c. relationships between a company and its investors
    d. a and c

3. Which of the following would improve a firm's return on investment?
    a. Raising sales prices and raising expenses
    b. Increasing earnings and investment in assets
    c. Lowering sales prices and increasing asset investment
    d. The answer cannot be determined from the information provided

4. Which of the following statements is **false**?
    a. A manager of a profit center has more responsibility than a manager of a cost center.
    b. A manager of an investment center has more responsibility than a manager of a cost center.
    c. A manager of a cost center has more responsibility than a manager of an investment center.
    d. A manager of an investment center has more responsibility than a manager of a profit center.

The following information applies to the next three questions: The 20X1 accounting records of Slamco, Inc. indicated that the company had revenues of $250,000, expenses of $150,000, and assets of $400,000.

5. Slamco's margin is:
    a. 60%
    b. 40%
    c. 62.5%
    d. 15%

6. Slamco's turnover is:
   a. .6 times
   b. .4 times
   c. .625 times
   d. .15 times

7. Slamco's return on investment is:
   a. 20%
   b. 25%
   c. 10%
   d. 15%

8. Sadona Company has a margin of 12% and a turnover of 3 times. Based on this information Sadona's return on investment is:
   a. 12%
   b. 30%
   c. 120%
   d. 36%

9. The electronic clock division of Time Company had budgeted sales of $750,000 and actual sales of $800,000. Budgeted expenses were $500,000 while actual expenses were $525,000. Based on this information, the responsibility report for the manager of this profit center would show:
   a. an unfavourable revenue variance
   b. a favourable cost variance
   c. a and b
   d. none of the above

10. Maxwell Taylor is responsible for generating revenues, controlling expenses and making purchases of capital assets. Mr. Taylor is an manager of:
    a. an asset center
    b. a profit center
    c. a capital center
    d. an investment center

11. Which of the following statements about ROI is true?
    a. ROI can be determined by dividing the net income by the amount of assets.
    b. ROI = Earned Income – Residual Income.
    c. ROI = margin x (1 – Tax Rate).
    d. none of the above.

12. Management by exception refers to a strategy that focuses on:
    a. highly successful managers
    b. unusual business opportunities
    c. significant variances
    d. centralized management

13. Belle Boutiques has an average rate of return of 12%. Details of a proposed investment include the following:

Sales Revenues	$20,000
Expenses	14,000
Cost of Asset	30,000

    Which of the following statements is accurate?
    a. The investment should be accepted because it will yield an ROI that is higher than the average ROI.
    b. Acceptance of the investment opportunity will yield residual income of $2,400.
    c. Acceptance of the investment opportunity will decrease the company wide ROI.
    d. both a and b.

14. The management of Data Industries obtained the following information about the performance of a major investment project:

Revenues	$200,000
Cost of Investment	300,000
Net Operating Income	48,000

    Assuming Data has a desired rate of return of 14%, the project's residual income was:
    a. $42,000
    b. $28,000
    c. $6,000
    d. None of the above

Exercise Type Problems

P1. The following information was drawn from an accounting report that was developed for a responsibility center that operated within the Gates Corporation. The actual volume of production and sales was 5,000 units.

	Standard	Actual
Per Unit Sales Data:		
Sales Price	$140	$134
Per Unit Variable Costs:	Standard	Actual
Materials Cost	$24	$26
Labour Cost	29	28
Overhead Cost	18	15
General, Selling and Administrative Cost	6	7
Fixed Costs:		
Manufacturing	$40,000	$38,000
General, Selling and Administrative	6,000	7,000

Required:
1. Determine the amount of the sales price variance and the cost variances. Also, indicate whether the variances are favourable or unfavourable.
2. Speculate as to whether the responsibility report applies to a cost center, profit center, or investment center. Provide a statement describing the rational for the type of center that you selected.

P1. Form for Requirement 1

	Gates Corporation Responsibility Report For 20X1			
	Budget	Actual	Variance	F or U
Sales Data:				
Sales Revenue				
Variable Costs:				
Materials				
Labour Cost				
Overhead Cost				
GS&A Cost				
Fixed Costs:				
Manufacturing				
GS&A				

P1. Form for Requirement 2

P2. Downey Company is organized into three investment divisions for the purpose of evaluating managerial performance. The truck rental division is managed by Rebecca Flynn. Flynn is responsible for the control of approximately $8,000,000 of operating assets. During the most recent accounting period, the truck rental division earned income of $1,200,000 on sales of $24,000,000. The company-wide return on investment (ROI) is approximately 11%.

Required:
1. Compute the margin for the truck rental division and explain what it means.
2. Compute the turnover for the truck rental division and explain what it means.
3. Compute the ROI for the truck rental division and comment on Flynn's performance.
4. Assume the Flynn is aware of a $2,000,000 investment opportunity that is expected to yield a 13% ROI. Assume further, that Downey rewards managers based on their division's ROI. Would you expect Flynn to accept or reject the investment opportunity? Explain your answer. Also, comment on how Flynn's decision to accept or reject the investment opportunity would affect the company's overall performance.
5. Suppose Downey changes its performance assessment measure from ROI to residual income (RI). Would you expect Flynn to accept or reject the investment opportunity described in Requirement 4? Support you answer with appropriate computations and commentary.

P2. Form for Requirement 1

Margin		
$\dfrac{\text{Net Income}}{\text{Sales}}$ =	_____ =	_____

P2. Form for Requirement 2

Turnover		
$\dfrac{\text{Sales}}{\text{Investment}}$ =	_____ =	_____

P2. Form for Requirement 3

Margin	x	Turnover	=	ROI
	x		=	

Alternatively, ROI can be calculated as follows:

ROI for Truck Rental Division
$\dfrac{\text{Net Income}}{\text{Investment}} = = $

P2. Form for Requirement 4

Truck Rental Division ROI with Additional Investment
$\dfrac{\text{Net Income}}{\text{Investment}} = = $

P2. Form for Requirement 5

Residual Income without Additional Investment					
Earned Income	-	(Investment x Desired ROI)		=	RI

Residual Income with Additional Investment					
Earned Income	-	(Investment x Desired ROI)		=	RI

P3. Perkin Pumps is a subsidiary of the Marrion Mechanical Company. Perkin makes pumps that are used to circulate water in swimming pools. Perkin purchases pump engines from Eleanor Engines, Inc. at a price of $120 per engine. Marrion recently purchased the Belmont Engine Company. Belmont is Eleanor's chief competitor in the pump engine business. Belmont claims that its pump engines are made of superior metals that result in longer life. At the current annual volume of production of 20,000 units, Belmont's accounting records indicate that the company incurs unit-level cost amounting to $70 per pump. Fixed product and facility-level costs amount to $400,000. Belmont sells its pumps at a price of $130 each. Belmont's current plant capacity would allow the company to produce up to 30,0000 pumps.

Marrion's CFO has asked Perkin's president to consider purchasing its engines from Belmont. Perkin's president acknowledges that Belmont engines are a suitable substitute for the engines that it currently purchases from Eleanor. However, he believes that the Belmont pumps are overpriced at $130. He is willing to pay no more than the $120 per engine (the price he is currently paying for Eleanor engines). In contrast, Belmont's president notes that other pump makers recognize the longer life value of Belmont engines and are willing to pay a premium for such quality. He states that Belmont is currently doing fine without selling to Perkin and is unwilling to sell to pumps for less than the current selling price of $130 per unit.

Required:
1. Since Perkin and Belmont are subsidiaries of the same parent company (Marrion), why would the presidents of the two divisions care about the sales price of the pumps? Whatever the price, are they not simply taking money out of one pocket and putting into another pocket of the same parent company?

2. If the presidents of Perkin and Belmont are unable to agree on a sales price, how will Marrion's profitability be affected? Quantify your answer assuming Perkin uses 6,000 pumps per year.

3. Given that the presidents of Perkin and Belmont cannot agree on a sales price, what other approaches could Marrion use to establish a transfer price?

P3. Form for Requirement 1

P3. Form for Requirement 2

Effect on Company-wide Profitability		
Cost to buy pumps from Eleanor		
Unit-level cost for Belmont to produce		
Difference		
x Annual volume		
Company savings if Perkin buys from Belmont		

P3. Form for Requirement 3

Multiple Choice Problems - Solutions

1. a

2. a

3. d To determine the impact on ROI, it would be necessary to know the amounts of the changes that are referenced in the answers. For example, answer "a" suggests that ROI would increase if sales prices and expenses increase. This would be true only if revenues increase more than the increase in expense. If expenses increase more than revenue, ROI would decline. Accordingly, the amounts of the increases must be known in order to determine the answer.

4. c A manager of an investment center is responsible revenue, cost and capital asset purchases. A manager of a cost center is responsible only for the control of cost.

5. b

Margin				
Net Income	=	$100,000	=	40%
Sales		$250,000		

6. c

Turnover				
Sales	=	$250,000	=	.625
Investment		$400,000		

7. b

Margin	x	Turnover	=	ROI
40%	x	.625	=	25%

Alternatively, ROI can be calculated as follows:

ROI for Truck Rental Division				
Net Income	=	$100,000	=	25%
Investment		$400,000		

8. d

Margin	x	Turnover	=	ROI
12%	x	3	=	36%

9. d Since the clock division earned more revenue than expected, the revenue variance is favourable. Since expenses were greater than expected, the cost variance is unfavourable.

10. d

11. a

12. c

13. d

ROI for Truck Rental Division				
Net Income / Investment	=	$6,000 / $30,000	=	20%

The investment ROI (20%) is higher than the company-wide rate (12%).

Residual Income				
Earned Income	-	(Investment x Desired ROI)	=	RI
$6,000	-	($30,000,000 x .12)	=	
$6,000	-	$3,600	=	$2,400

14. c

Residual Income				
Earned Income	-	(Investment x Desired ROI)	=	RI
$48,000	-	($300,000 x .14)	=	
$48,000	-	$42,000	=	$6,000

Exercise Type Problems - Solutions

P1. Solution for Requirements 1

Gates Corporation Responsibility Report For 20X1				
	Budget	Actual	Variance	F or U
Sales Data:				
Sales Revenue	$700,000	$670,000	$30,000	U
Variable Costs:				
Materials	120,000	130,000	10,000	U
Labour Cost	145,000	140,000	5,000	F
Overhead Cost	90,000	75,000	15,000	F
GS&A Cost	30,000	35,000	5,000	U
Fixed Costs:				
Manufacturing	40,000	38,000	2,000	F
GS&A	6,000	7,000	1,000	U

P1. Solution for Requirement 2

Since the report includes both revenue and expense items, it appears to apply to a profit center. A report for a cost center would contain only cost items. A report for an investment center would likely contain information regarding capital investment activity as well as revenue and expense items.

P2. Solution for Requirement 1

Margin				
Net Income	=	$1,200,000	=	5%
Sales		$24,000,000		

The **margin** shows the percentage of each sales dollar that is profit. In this case, the truck rental division earns a five-cent profit on each dollar of sales it generates.

P2. Solution for Requirement 2

Turnover				
Sales	=	$24,000,000	=	3
Investment		$8,000,000		

The **turnover** shows the number of sales dollars generated for each dollar of investment. In this case, the truck rental division generates three dollar of sales for each dollar it invests.

P2. Solution for Requirement 3

Margin	x	Turnover	=	ROI
5%	x	3	=	15%

Alternatively, ROI can be calculated as follows:

ROI for Truck Rental Division				
Net Income	=	$1,200,000	=	15%
Investment		$8,000,000		

Since the truck rental division's ROI (15%) is higher than the company-wide rate (11%), Flynn appears to be outperforming the other company managers.

P2. Solution for Requirement 4

Truck Rental Division ROI with Additional Investment				
Net Income	=	$1,200,000 + $260,000*	=	14.6%
Investment		$8,000,000 + $2,000,000		

*Net income from additional investment:
$2,000,000 x .13 = $260,000

Since the additional investment would lower the truck rental division's ROI (15% versus 14.6%), Flynn would likely reject the investment opportunity. The rejection of the investment opportunity would lead to suboptomization, because the expected return is higher than the company wide ROI (15% versus 11%).

P2. Solution for Requirement 5

Residual Income without Additional Investment				
Earned Income	-	(Investment x Desired ROI)	=	RI
$1,200,000	-	($8,000,000 x .11)	=	
$1,200,000	-	$880,000	=	$320,000

Residual Income with Additional Investment				
Earned Income	-	(Investment x Desired ROI)	=	RI
$1,200,000 + $260,000*	-	($10,000,000 x .11)	=	
$1,460,000	-	$1,100,000	=	$360,000

*Net income from additional investment:
$2,000,000 x .13 = $260,000

If Flynn accepts the investment opportunity, her residual income will increase by $40,000 ($360,000 – $320,000). Using residual income to evaluate managerial performance will eliminate the motivation for suboptomization because accepting the investment opportunity will benefit both Flynn and the company as a whole.

P3. Solution for Requirement 1

It is true that the intercompany sales price of the pumps will have no impact on the parent company's earnings. However, the presidents of Perkin and Belmont are accountable for the profitability of their relative divisions. If Perkin purchases pumps from Belmont, the sales price represents not only revenue to Belmont, but cost to Perkin. Belmont benefits most from a higher transfer price; Perkin benefits most from a lower transfer price.

P3. Solution for Requirement 2

Marrion will be less profitable if Perkin continues to purchase engines from Eleanor at $120 each than from Belmont regardless of the transfer price. From the parent company's point of view, the question is whether to make pumps internally (have Belmont produce them), or outsource them (buy from Eleanor). Because Belmont's product-level and facility-level costs will be incurred in either case, they are not avoidable and therefore are not relevant. An analysis of the relevant information follows:

Effect on Company-wide Profitability		
Cost to buy pumps from Eleanor	$ 120	per unit
Unit-level cost for Belmont to produce	(70)	per unit
Difference	$ 50	per unit
x Annual volume	x 6,000	units
Company savings if Perkin buys from Belmont	$300,000	total

P3. Solution for Requirement 3

Since Belmont has excess capacity, any transfer price greater than the unit-level cost to produce pumps ($70) will increase Belmont's profitability. At the same time, Perkin will be more profitable if it is able to buy pumps for any transfer price less than it currently pays for Eleanor pumps ($120). Marrion management could insist that the two presidents negotiate a transfer price, or it could arbitrarily set a reasonable price and force the intercompany sales. However, senior-level managers must be cautious about employing these alternatives because either could damage morale. The long-term benefits of permitting autonomous management may outweigh the short-term savings computed above.

Chapter 10
Planning for Capital Investments

Learning Objectives for the Chapter

The material in this chapter of the study guide is designed to facilitate your ability to:

- Distinguish between capital investments and investments in stocks and bonds.
- Understand and apply the concept of time value of money to capital investment decisions.
- Distinguish between return on investment and recovery of investment.
- Explain why the cost of capital constitutes the minimum acceptable rate of return for a capital investment.
- Use present value tables to determine the present value of future cash flows.
- Distinguish between lump-sum payments and ordinary annuities.
- Appreciate the power of computer software in determining present values.
- Understand the reinvestment assumption implicit in the interest tables and computer software.
- Determine and interpret the net present value of an investment opportunity.
- Determine the internal rate of return of an investment opportunity.
- Identify the typical cash inflows and outflows associated with capital investments.
- Determine the payback period for an investment opportunity.
- Determine the unadjusted rate of return for an investment opportunity.
- Conduct a post-audit of an investment that has been exercised.

Brief Explanation of the Learning Objectives

Distinguish between capital investments and investments in stocks and bonds.

Capital investments involve the acquisition of assets that must be used in the operation of a business in order to recover the money invested and make a profit. They may be thought of as active investments, whereas the purchase of stocks and bonds may be thought of as passive investments. However, the present value techniques used to evaluate capital investments can also be used to evaluate investments in stocks and bonds.

Understand and apply the concept of time value of money to capital investment decisions.

Simply stated, the concept of the time value of money refers to the fact that a dollar received today is worth more than a dollar received in the future because today's dollar can be invested and will be worth more than a dollar in the future. Time value of money principles are used to help compare the future dollars generated by a capital investment to the current dollars that must be spent if the capital project is accepted. Several of the self-study problems are designed to help you achieve this objective more fully.

Distinguish between return on investment and recovery of investment.

Getting back the money initially invested in a capital project, after adjusting for the time value of money, is simply *recovery of the investment*. While this is important, businesses want to get back more than their initial investment; they want to earn a profit, which represents a *return on their investment*.

Explain why the cost of capital constitutes the minimum acceptable rate of return for a capital investment.

To invest in a capital project a company must first obtain the funds necessary for the initial investment. There is a cost of obtaining these funds that may be explicit and/or implicit. Explicit costs include out-of-pocket costs, such as those needed to pay interest on borrowed funds. Implicit costs include opportunity costs, such as the money that will not be earned if cash is taken out of an interest bearing account and invested in a capital project. A company's *cost of capital* includes its implicit and explicit costs of obtaining money. A business would not want to invest funds that cost 10% to obtain in an investment that earned only 9%. Thus, the minimum acceptable return for a project is at least equal to the company's cost of capital.

Use present value tables to determine the present value of future cash flows.

Several of the self-study problems are designed to help you achieve this objective more fully.

Distinguish between lump-sum payments and ordinary annuities.

A lump-sum payment is a payment of a given dollar amount that occurs only once. An annuity is a series of payments with very specific characteristics. To be an annuity, the payments must be of exactly equal amounts, at exactly fixed time-intervals, and must occur in an investment situation with a constant rate of return. An example of an annuity would be the payment of $10,000 on December 31, of each of the next ten years into an account that earns 7% compounded annually. An annuity problem can be solved as if it were a series of lump-sum payments, but a series of unequal lump-sum payments cannot be solved as n annuity.

Appreciate the power of computer software in determining present values.

Software programs offer an efficient means of converting future values into present value equivalents. These programs are frequently built into hand-held calculators and computer spreadsheet programs such as Microsoft Excel. As well, the instantaneous conversion power of the spreadsheet is extremely useful in answering what-if questions.

Understand the reinvestment assumption implicit in the interest tables and computer software.

When a company invest in a capital project it expects to receive cash inflows from that investment throughout its life. What do accountants assume happens to the money received? They assume the money is reinvested. If a company is computing the net present value of a project, then the assumption is that these receipts are reinvested at the rate used to compute the present value of the cash flows, which should be at least equal to the company's cost of capital. If the internal rate of return of an investment is being computed, then the receipts are assumed to be reinvested at the internal rate of return generated by that investment project. The assumption that cash received from a project is reinvested at the rate being used from the interest tables is an essential element of the compounding of interest concept.

Determine and interpret the net present value of an investment opportunity.

Several of the self-study problems are designed to help you achieve this objective more fully.

Determine the internal rate of return of an investment opportunity.

Several of the self-study problems are designed to help you achieve this objective more fully.

Identify the typical cash inflows and outflows associated with capital investments.

Cash **outflows** for a capital investment typically include:
    The initial investment in assets such as buildings and equipment. However, the initial investment can also be for such costs as those needed to train employees.
    The investment in additional working capital items, such as inventory or accounts

receivables. Working capital investments are usually assumed to occur at the beginning of an investment project, but they can occur at any time.

Cash operating expenses that are incurred to keep the project going (incremental expenses). These would include such costs as the wages of new employees hired as a result of the capital project. For computational purposes, incremental expenses are usually subtracted from incremental revenues, and the resulting net cash flow (or incremental cash flow) is used.

Major overhauls of equipment during the life of the investment project. These costs could be treated as incremental expenses, but for financial reporting purposes, they might be <u>capitalized</u> when incurred rather than <u>expensed.</u>

Cash **inflows** from a capital investment typically include:

Revenues generated by the project (incremental revenues).

Reductions in the costs that would otherwise be incurred if the capital project is not accepted (cost savings).

Salvage value of any new assets acquired for the project. These typically occur at the end of the project.

Salvage value of any old assets sold if they are replaced by new assets acquired for the project. Note that the salvage value of these old assets is usually recovered at the beginning of the new investment, so they are typically subtracted from the initial investment, thus reducing cash outflows, rather than being treated as separate cash inflows. This is especially true if the salvage value of the old asset is used as a trade-in value against the cost of the new assets acquired.

Recovery of working capital invested in the project. These cash inflows typically occur at the end of the investment, and they are usually assumed to equal 100% of the working capital initially invested.

Determine the payback period for an investment opportunity.

The payback period of a project is the time it takes the company to get back an amount of cash that equals the initial cash invested in the project. Several of the self-study problems are designed to help you achieve this objective more fully.

Determine the unadjusted rate of return for an investment opportunity.

The preferred method for computing the unadjusted rate of return is:

$$\frac{\text{Average incremental increase in annual net income}}{\text{Average book value of the investment}}$$

Note that the unadjusted rate of return is the only method presented in this chapter that uses *accrual based earnings* in its computation. The other three methods are all based on the analysis of cash information. Several of the self-study problems are designed to help you achieve this objective more fully.

Conduct a post-audit of an investment that has been exercised.

Deciding whether or not a capital investment opportunity should be accepted requires making many estimates and assumptions about future events. The events that actually occur will certainly not be exactly like those anticipated. A postaudit involves recalculating the capital project's net present value, internal rate of return, etc., based on the actual events that occurred. The purpose of this exercise is to improve the accuracy of future capital investment planning activities.

Self-Study Problems

Multiple-Choice Problems

1. Which of the following statements is true?
   a. An advantage of the payback method is that it considers the time value of money.
   b. The internal rate of return of a project will be equal to its unadjusted rate of return.
   c. If an investment opportunity is acceptable based on its net present value, it will also be acceptable based on its internal rate of return.
   d. All methods of capital planning are based on cash flows only.

2. Indicate which of the following statements is **false**.
   a. Using a lower the interest rate to compute the present value of an investment's future cash flows, will cause the present value of those cash flows will be higher.
   b. An investment opportunity should be rejected if its internal rate of return is higher than the company's cost of capital.
   c. The further into the future a cash flow occurs, the lower the its present value will be.
   d. A company's minimum desired rate of return should never be less than its cost of capital.

3. Ralph Jones' friend is retiring and has offered to sell Ralph his existing newsstand, Stuff In Print, (SIP) that is located in the local airport. All of the equipment at SIP is rented, so all of SIP's expenses and revenues are in cash. The license to operate SIP expires in eight years, so Ralph assumes he would operate the business for only eight years if he buys it. The annual net cash flow for SIP is expected to be $75,000. If Ralph needs to earn at least 10% on his investment, what is the maximum amount he should pay for SIP?
   a. $ 34,988
   b. $400,119
   c. $503,256
   d. $600,000

4. Lisa Plander, who is 25 yeas old, wishes to retire with $1,000,000 when she is 45. To accomplish this Lisa is going to ask her grandmother for a "nest egg." Assuming she invests the money her grandmother gives her in a mutual fund that is expected to earn 10%, how much money must she get from granny if she hopes to meet her early retirement goal?
   a. $161,506
   b. $117,458
   c. $ 42,568
   d. $148,644

5. Linda Garcia makes pottery and is considering the purchase of a new kiln. The kiln would cost $7,500, and should last five years, at which time it will have no salvage value. Linda would incur $1,000 of annual cash expenses to operate the kiln, but she would avoid $3,500 of costs she has been incurring annually to rent space in other potters' kilns. Linda uses straight-line amortization, and her tax rate is 30%. What is the annual net cash flow, after taxes, related to acquiring the new kiln versus continuing to rent kiln space?
   a. $2,200
   b. $2,500
   c. $1,800
   d. $ 700

6. Carplex Inc. is considering replacing an existing machine with a new machine that is more efficient. The following information is available for the proposed project, which has a life of five years.

Cost of new machine	$100,000
Salvage value of new machine at the end of year 5	15,000
Book value of the existing machine	70,000
Trade-in value of existing machine	20,000
Annual cost savings of new machine	18,000
Minimum desired rate of return	12%

   What is the net present value of this investment project?
   a. $18,072
   b. $43,397
   c. $(8,765)
   d. $(6,603)

7. Sarah Ramarez, a freshman at State University, is considering starting a business in her dorm room that would sell computer supplies such as diskettes and ink cartridges to her fellow students. Sarah estimates the business would generate 1,500 in net cash flows each of the next four years. To start the business she would need to acquire a computer that cost $2,000, and has an estimated salvage value of $500 at the end of four years. She also must spend $4,000 for inventory items; all of this money will be recovered at the end of year four. Sarah's cost of capital is 9%.

   What is the net present value of this investment opportunity?
   a. $(786)
   b. $1,694
   c. $2,048
   d. $8,048

8. Discovery Labs is considering acquiring new equipment that management estimates will reduce its cash operating expenses by $50,000 each year for the next five years. After five years the company believes the equipment will be technologically obsolete and will have no salvage value. The equipment will costs $180,000 and the company will have to spend $20,000 immediately to train its staff to use the new equipment.

    What is the internal rate of return of this investment project?
    a. 25%
    b. 12%
    c. 8%
    d. 5%

9. Marc Solomon is trying to sell his business. To acquire the company, Jamie Watkins has offered to made the following payments to Marc:

    $ 80,000 per year for the next nine years, and a "balloon payment" of $1,080,000 at the end of year 10.

    If Marc believes 8% is the minimum rate of return he should use when evaluating investment decisions, what is today's value of Jamie's offer?
    a. $ 999,999
    b. $ 833,747
    c. $ 962,944
    d. $1,800,000

The Following Information Pertains to the Next Two Questions:
Phoenix Company has been offered an investment opportunity that, if accepted, will require an initial expenditure of $100,000 to acquire a new machine. The machine has an expected life of eight years and no salvage value. Phoenix uses straight-line deprecation. Annual cash revenues from the project are estimated to be $20,000, while annual cash expenses are estimated to be $4,000.

10. What is the payback period of this investment project (rounded to the nearest year)?
    a. 6 years
    b. 8 years
    c. 5 years
    d. 29 years

11. What is the unadjusted rate of return of this investment project?
    a. 16.0%
    b. 7.5%
    c. 8.0%
    d. 7.0%

The Following Information Pertains to the Next Two Questions:
Jimmy Wilde lives in an area of the west that is becoming a popular tourist destination. Jimmy is considering starting an off-road jeep-tour business by purchasing a four wheel drive jeep. Because he plans to work from his house, the jeep is the only asset he will need to purchase. The jeep will cost $20,000 and will have a life of five years and no expected salvage value. Jimmy will use the straight-line amortization method. Jimmy estimates the net cash flows of the business for the next five years will be as follow:

Year	Net Cash Flow
1	$6,000
2	8,000
3	7,000
4	6,000
5	5,000

12. What is the unadjusted rate of return of this investment?
    a. 12%
    b. 24%
    c. 60%
    d. 64%

13. What is the payback period of this investment project (rounded to the nearest year)?
    a. 2 years
    b. 3 years
    c. 4 years
    d. more than 5 years

14. Will Su was injured in a traffic accident, which was not his fault. The insurance company of the driver responsible for the accident has offered Will any one of the following four options to settle the case. Whichever option Will chooses, he plans to invest the money received in an account that pays an annual interest rate of 8%.

    Option 1:
    $65,000 paid immediately.
    Option 2:
    $16,000 paid annually for five years, beginning one year from today.
    Option 3:
    $10,000 paid annually for ten years, beginning one year from today.
    Option 4:
    $4,800 paid semiannually for the ten years, beginning six months from today.

    Which option should Will accept?
    a. Option 1
    b. Option 2
    c. Option 3

d. Option 4

15. The following information is available for four projects under consideration at Ventures Limited.

    Project 1:
    This project has an internal rate of return of 12%. Venture Limited's cost of capital is 10%.

    Project 2:
    This project has a payback period of four years. Venture Limited's minimum acceptable payback period is five years.

    Project 3:
    This project has an unadjusted rate of return of 12%. Venture Limited's cost of capital is 10%.

    Project 4:
    This project has a net present value of $-0-, which was computed using factors in the 10% columns of the present value tables.

    Based only on the information above, and assuming only one project can be accepted, which project would you recommend that Venture Limited accept?
    a. Project 1
    b. Project 2
    c. Project 3
    d. Project 4

Exercise Type Problems

P1. Custom Cabinets is considering acquiring a machine that will reduce the labour time and cost needed to make cabinets. The machine cost $100,000, has an estimated life of eight years, and an expected salvage value of $20,000. If purchased, the machine is expected to replace labour cost by $15,000 per year. Custom Cabinets wants to earn at least 7% on its investments. The company uses the straight-line amortization method, and has a tax rate of 40%.

Required:

1. Compute the <u>before-tax</u> net present value of the investment opportunity.

2. Compute the <u>after-tax</u> net present value of the investment opportunity.

3. Compute the <u>after-tax</u> unadjusted rate of return for the investment opportunity.

P1. Use the following form to develop information to be used for completing all three requirements.

Annual before-tax cost savings on labour	$
– Amortization expense	
Increase in income before-taxes	
– Income taxes	
Increase in net income	$
Increase in cash inflows, before-taxes	$
– Tax expenses	
Increase in cash inflows, after-taxes	$

P1. Form for Requirement 1.

Increase in cash inflows, before-taxes	$	
x Present value factor		
Present value of annual cash inflows, before taxes		$
Salvage value		
x Present value factor		
Present value of salvage value		
Present value of all cash inflows		
– Initial investment		
Net present value of the project, before-taxes		$

P1. Form for Requirement 2.

Increase in cash inflows, after-taxes	$	
x Present value factor		
Present value of annual cash inflows, after taxes		$
Salvage value		
x Present value factor		
Present value of salvage value		
Present value of all cash inflows		
– Initial investment		
Net present value of the project, after-taxes		$

P1. Form for Requirement 3.

Increase in net income	$	
÷ Average investment	$	
= Unadjusted rate of return		_____ %

P2. About five years ago Seatback Industries evaluated an investment opportunity using the net present value method. At that time the projected cash flows were:

Initial investment	$500,000

Year	Projected Net Cash Inflows
1	$150,000
2	150,000
3	150,000
4	150,000
5	150,000
Total	$750,000

After analyzing the investment, using a rate of return of 14%, Seatback's president decided to go forward with the proposed project. The project has recently been completed and the total cash flows generated were a bit more than had been projected, but the timing of the cash flows was not the same as forecasted.

Actual cash flows for the project were:

Initial investment	$500,000

Year	Actual Net Cash Inflows
1	$ 80,000
2	120,000
3	150,000
4	220,000
5	200,000
Total	$770,000

The company's president has assigned you the task of doing a postaudit of the project to determine if things turned out as well as planned.

Required:

1. Compute the net present value of the projected based on Seatback's original estimates.
2. Compute the net present value of the project based on the cash flows that actually occurred.
3. Comment briefly about why the actual net present value was not equal to the projected net present value.

P2. Form for Requirement 1

Annuity of annual cash inflows	$
x Present value factor from Table 2	
Present value of net cash inflows	
- Initial investment	
Projected net present value of the project	$

P2. Form for Requirement 2

Year	Cash Inflow (Outflow)	Present Value Factor	Present Value of Cash Flow
1	$ 80,000		$
2	120,000		
3	150,000		
4	220,000		
5	200,000		
Totals	$ 770,000		
Initial Investment	$(500,000)		
Net Present Value of Project			$

P2. Form for Requirement 3.

_____

_____

_____

_____

_____

_____

Multiple Choice Problems - Solutions

1. c. Both the net present value method and the internal rate of return method take into consideration the time value of money. If the net present value of an investment opportunity is positive when computed using a company's cost of capital, then the internal rate of return for that same project will be higher than the company's cost of capital.

2. b. If the internal rate of return for an investment opportunity is higher than the company's cost of capital, then the project should be accepted.

3. b. Present value of annual cost savings ($50,000 x 5.334926) = $400,119
   [Table 2: n = 8; i = 10%]

4. d. Present value of $1,000,000 received 20 years in the future ($1,000,000 x 0.148644) = $148,644
   [Table 1: n = 20; i = 10%]

5. a.
Rent payment avoided	$ 3,500
- New operating costs	(1,000)
Increase in before tax cash inflows	2,500
- Amortization expense ($7,500 ÷ 5 years)	(1,500)
Increase in taxable income	1,000
x Income tax rate	.30
Increase in income tax expense	$ 300
Increase in cash flows before taxes (see above)	$ 2,500
- Increase in income taxes	300
Increase in annual cash flows - after taxes	$ 2,200

6. d.
Present value of annual cost savings ($18,000 x 3.604776)	$64,886
[Table 2: n = 5; i = 12%]	
+ Present value of salvage value of new machine ($15,000 x .567427)	8,511
[Table 1: n = 5; i = 12%]	
Present value of future cash inflows	73,397
- Initial investment ($100,000 ! $20,000)	80,000
Net present value of the project	$(6,603)

7. c.
Present value of cash inflows:		
Present value of annual inflow from sales ($1,500 x 3.239720)		$4,860
[Table 2: n = 4; i = 9%]		
Present value of salvage value of the computer ($500 x .708425)		354
[Table 1: n = 4; i = 9%]		
Present value of recovery of working capital ($4,000 x .708425)		2,834
[Table 1: n = 4; i = 9%]		
Total		8,048
Present value of cash outflows:		
Purchase price of computer ($2,000 x 1.0)	$2,000	
Expenditure for working capital ($4,000 x 1.0)	4,000	
Total		(6,000)
Net present value of the investment opportunity		$2,048

8. c. (Present value factor from Table 2 [n = 5; i = ?%]) x $50,000 = $180,000 + $20,000
Present value factor from Table 2 [n = 5; i = ?%] = $200,000) $50,000
Present value factor from Table 2 [n = 5; i = ?%] = 4.000
Present value factor from Table 2 where n = 5 and i = 8% = 3.992710
Therefore, the internal rate of return for the proposed project is 8%.

9. a. There are two ways to solve this problem:

Option 1:
Present value of annual payment for years 1 through 9 ($80,000 x 6.246888) $499,751
    [Table 2: n = 9; i = 8%]
Present value of the balloon payment ($1,080,000 x .463193)   500,248
    [Table 1: n = 10; i = 8%]
Total $999,999

Option 2:
Present value of annual payment for years 1 through 10 ($80,000 x 6.710081) $536,806
    [Table 2: n = 10; i = 8%]
Present value of $1,000,000 of the balloon payment ($1,000,000 x .463193)   463,193
    [Table 1: n = 10; i = 8%]
Total $999,999

Note: Students who studied present value concepts in their first accounting course should note the similarity of the computations required to solve this investment problem compared to those used in Financial Accounting to compute the selling price of bonds payable. The similarity is especially evident in the solution presented in Option 2. The answer above would be $1,000,000 if the factors in the present value tables were carried out one more decimal place. A bond payable with a face value of $1,000,000 and a stated interest rate of 8%, would pay the holder $80,000 interest per year.

10. a. Initial investment $100,000
÷ Increase in annual net cash inflows ($20,000 - $4,000) $16,000

= Payback period   6.25 years

11. d. Increase in annual net cash flows ($20,000 - $4,000) $16,000
- Amortization expense ($100,000 ÷ 8 years)   12,500
Increase in annual net earnings $ 3,500

Increase in annual net earnings $ 3,500
÷ Average investment ($100,000 ÷ 2) $50,000

= Unadjusted return on investment   7.0%

12. b.

Year	Net Cash Flow	−	Amortization Expense (#)	=	Net Earnings
1	$6,000		$4,000		$ 2,000
2	8,000		4,000		4,000
3	7,000		4,000		3,000
4	6,000		4,000		2,000
5	5,000		4,000		1,000
Total					$12,000

\# Amortization expense = $20,000 ÷ 5 years = $4,000.

Unadjusted rate of return:
    Average annual net income ($12,000 ÷ 5 years) $2,400
    Average investment ($20,000 ÷ 2) $10,000

Unadjusted rate of return = 24%

13. b.

Year	Net Cash Flow	Cumulative Cash Flows
1	$6,000	$ 6,000
2	8,000	14,000
3	7,000	21,000 **
4	6,000	27,000
5	5,000	32,000

** The cumulative cash flows are approximately equal to the initial investment of $20,000 after three years.

14. c. To solve this problem, the net present value of each option must be computed, and the option with the highest net present value is the best.

The present value of Option 1 is $65,000.
The present value of Option 2 is $63,883. $16,000 x 3.992710 [Table 2: n = 5; i = 8%]
The present value of Option 3 is $67,101. $10,000 x 6.710081 [Table 2: n = 10; i = 8%]
The present value of Option 4 is $65,234. $4,800 x 13.590326 [Table 2: n = 20; i = 4%]

15. a. Even though projects 1, 2, and 3 meet the company's minimum investment criteria, if only one project must be selected as the best, it should be project 1. This is because projects 2 and 3 were analyzed using methods that do not consider the time value of money, Project 1 was found acceptable using the internal rate of return method, which does take into consideration the time value of money. Project 4 was also analyzed using a method that considers the time value of money, but because it has a $-0- net present value, it is not as acceptable as a project that has an internal rate of return 2% above the company's cost of capital

Exercise Type Problems

P1. The information is used for completing all three requirements.

Annual before-tax cost savings on labour	$15,000
- Amortization expense [($100,000 - $20,000) ÷ 8]	10,000
Increase in income before-taxes	5,000
- Income taxes ($5,000 x .40)	(2,000)
Increase in net income	$ 3,000
Increase in cash inflows, before-taxes	$15,000
– Tax expenses	(2,000)
Increase in cash inflows, after-taxes	$13,000

P1. Requirement 1.

Increase in cash inflows, before-taxes	$15,000	
x Present value factor [Table 2: n = 8; i =7%]	5.971229	
Present value of annual cash inflows, before taxes		$ 89,569
Salvage value	20,000	
x Present value factor [Table 1: n = 8; i =7%]	0.582009	
Present value of salvage value		11,640
Present value of all cash inflows		101,209
- Initial investment		(100,000)
Net present value of project, before-taxes		$ 1,209

P1. Requirement 2.

Increase in cash inflows, after-taxes	$13,000	
x Present value factor [Table 2: n = 8; i =7%]	5.971229	
Present value of annual cash inflows, after taxes		$ 77,626
Salvage value	20,000	
x Present value factor [Table 1: n = 8; i =7%]	0.582009	
Present value of salvage value		11,640
Present value of all cash inflows		89,266
- Initial investment		(100,000)
Net present value of project, after-taxes		$ (10,734)

P1. Requirement 3.

Increase in net income	$ 3,000
÷ Average investment {($100,000 - $20,000) ÷ 2}	$40,000
= Unadjusted rate of return	7.5%

P2. Requirement 1.

Annuity of annual cash inflows	$ 150,000
x Present value factor from Table 2 (n = 5; i = 14%)	3.433081
Present value of net cash inflows	514,962
– Initial investment	(500,000)
Projected net present value of the project	$ 14,962

P2. Requirement 2.

Year	Cash Inflow (Outflow)	Present Value Factor	Present Value of Cash Flow
1	$ 80,000	0.877193	$ 70,175
2	120,000	0.769468	92,336
3	150,000	0.674972	101,238
4	220,000	0.592080	130,258
5	200,000	0.519369	103,874
Totals	$770,000		497,881
Initial Investment	$(500,000)	1.000000	(500,000)
Net Present Value of Project			$(2,119)

P2. Requirement 3.

Even though the actual cash inflows were $20,000 greater than projected ($770,000 - $750,000) the net present value of the project based on these cash flows was significantly less than projected. This resulted from the timing of the cash inflows. The majority actual cash inflows occurred in the later years of the project, rather than evenly over its life, as had been projected.

Chapter 11
Product Costing in Service and Manufacturing Entities

Learning Objectives for the Chapter

The material in this chapter of the study guide is designed to facilitate your ability to:

- Understand the need for service and product cost information.
- Understand how product costs flow from raw materials, to work in process, to finished goods, and ultimately to cost of goods sold.
- Distinguish between costing for service versus manufacturing entities.
- Demonstrate how product cost flow affects financial statements through a horizontal financial statements model.
- Understand the necessity of assigning estimated overhead costs to the inventory and cost of goods sold accounts during an accounting period.
- Record applied and actual overhead costs in a manufacturing overhead account.
- Record product costs in T-accounts.
- Understand the cyclical nature of product cost flows.
- Comprehend the relationship between over- or underapplied overhead and variance analysis.
- Prepare a schedule of cost of goods manufactured and sold.
- Prepare a set of financial statements for a manufacturing entity.
- Distinguish between absorption and variable costing.

Brief Explanation of the Learning Objectives

Understand the need for service and product cost information.

Product and service cost information is used in financial reporting, managerial accounting, and contract negotiations.

- **Financial Reporting.** Companies are required by generally accepted accounting principles (GAAP) to show service and product costs in their public financial reports. For example, the cost of manufacturing products must be allocated between cost of goods sold which is shown on the income statement and ending inventory which is shown on the balance sheet.

- **Managerial Reporting.** Service and product cost information is used for planning purposes in the budgeting process, for cost control, and pricing decisions.

- **Negotiations.** Service and product cost information may be used by governmental agencies to enforce regulatory requirements and in the execution of cost-plus contracts.

Understand how product costs flow from raw materials, to work in process, to finished goods, and ultimately to cost of goods sold.

Most manufacturing companies accumulate their product costs in three distinct inventory accounts: (1) raw materials which includes lumber, metals, paints, chemicals, etc. that will be used to make the company's products; (2) work in process which includes partially completed products; and (3) finished goods which includes fully processed products that are ready for sale. The cost of materials is first recorded in a raw materials inventory account. The cost of materials placed in production is then transferred from the raw materials inventory account to a work in process inventory account. The cost of labour and overhead are added to the work in process inventory account. The cost of goods completed during the period is transferred from the work in process inventory account to the finished goods inventory account. The cost of the goods that are sold during the accounting period is transferred from the finished goods inventory account to the cost of goods sold account. The balances that remain in the raw materials, work in process, and finished goods inventory accounts appear on the balance sheet. The amount of product cost transferred to the cost of goods sold account is expensed on the income statement.

Distinguish between costing for service versus manufacturing entities.

Like manufacturing companies, many service companies have costs that start with raw materials and pass through production stages such as work in process, finished goods, and cost of goods sold. The distinguishing feature between service and manufacturing companies is that products of service companies are consumed immediately. In other words, services cannot be stored and sold at a later time. As a result, service companies will not have work in process and finished goods inventory accounts wherein costs are stored before being transferred to a cost of goods sold account.

Demonstrate how product cost flow affects financial statements through a horizontal financial statements model.

You should be able to explain how the recognition product costs affects the balance sheet, income statement, and cash flow statement by recording cost flow transactions in a financial statement model like the one that is shown below. In the cash column, you should be able to distinguish cash flow transactions as being inflows or outflows and to categorize those transactions as financing, investing, or operating transactions.

	Assets			=	Liab.	+ Equity	Rev.	−	Exp.	= Net Inc.	Cash Flow
	Raw Materials	+ Work in Process	+ Finished Goods								
1	−	+	n/a	=	n/a	n/a	n/a	−	n/a	= n/a	n/a
2	n/a	−	+	=	n/a	n/a	n/a	−	n/a	= n/a	n/a
3	n/a	n/a	−	=	n/a	−	n/a	−	+	= −	n/a

Understand the necessity of assigning estimated overhead costs to the inventory and cost of goods sold accounts during an accounting period.

Many costs that benefit production at one point in time are incurred at a different point in time. For example, the cost of manufacturing supplies used to make products during an accounting period, may not be known until the end of the accounting period. To ensure that products are charged with the costs incurred to make them, it is frequently necessary to recognize an estimated cost at the time the products are being produced. For example, an estimated amount of supply cost is included in the determination of the product cost at the time of production. Adjustments for differences between estimated and actual costs are made at the end of the accounting period when actual costs are known.

Record applied and actual overhead costs in a manufacturing overhead account.

The manufacturing overhead account is a temporary account that is used to provide a fair allocation of overhead costs to products as they are being manufactured. Rational allocation is used to determine the amount of overhead cost to assign to products during the manufacturing process. More specifically, overhead costs are assigned to work in process via the use of a **predetermined overhead rate** which is calculated as follows:

$$\text{Predetermined Overhead Rate} = \frac{\text{Total Estimated Overhead Cost}}{\text{Allocation Base (Cost Driver)}}$$

The entry to record the allocated cost includes a debit (increase) to the work in process account and a credit (decrease) to the manufacturing overhead account. Actual costs are recorded as debits (increases) to the manufacturing overhead account. If the applied overhead cost is greater than the actual overhead cost, the differences is called **overapplied overhead**. If the applied overhead cost is less than the actual overhead cost, the difference is called **underapplied overhead**. The amount of over or under applied overhead is closed to the cost of goods sold account at the end of the accounting period.

Record product costs in T-accounts.

Product costs normally pass through several asset accounts prior to being expensed as cost of goods sold. Transfers from one asset account to another (e.g., raw materials to work in process or work in process to finished goods) are asset exchange transactions. Entries to recognize these asset exchange transactions are recorded by crediting (decreasing) the asset account from which the costs are being transferred and debiting (increasing) the asset account in which the costs are being placed. At the point of sale, product costs are transferred from the finished goods inventory account (asset) to the cost of goods sold account (expense). This transfer is an asset use transaction that is recorded by crediting (decreasing) the finished goods inventory account and debiting (increasing) the cost of goods sold account which decreases net income and ultimately retained earnings.

Comprehend the relationship between over- or underapplied overhead and variance analysis.

The amount of estimated cost and volume used to compute the predetermined overhead rate are drawn from a company's standard cost data. Accordingly, the predetermined overhead rate is a representation of the standard overhead cost. As a result, the amount of over or underapplied overhead is a variance (difference between standard overhead and actual overhead).

Prepare a schedule of cost of goods manufactured and sold.

To facilitate the analytical process, the product cost information is summarized in a *schedule* that explains the determination of the cost of goods manufactured and sold. The schedule is an internal document that does not appear in a company's published financial statements. However, the result of the schedule (i.e., cost of goods sold) does appear in the income statement. An example **schedule of cost of goods manufactured and sold** is shown on the following page.

ABC Manufacturing Company
Cost of Goods Manufactured and Sold
For Period Ended 12/31/20X2

Beginning Raw Materials Inventory	$XXX
Plus: Purchases	XXX
Raw Materials Available for Use	XXX
Less: Ending Raw Materials Inventory	XXX
Direct Raw Materials Used	XXX
Direct Labour	XXX
Manufactured Overhead Applied	XXX
Total Manufacturing Costs	XXX
Plus: Beginning Work in process Inventory	XXX
Total Work in process Inventory	XXX
Less: Ending Work in process Inventory	XXX
Cost of Goods Manufactured	XXX
Plus: Beginning Finished Goods Inventory	XXX
Cost of Goods Available for Sale	XXX
Less: Ending Finished Goods Inventory	XXX
Cost of Goods Sold - Unadjusted	XXX
Plus Underapplied Overhead	XXX
Cost of Goods Sold - Actual	XXX

Prepare a set of financial statements for a manufacturing entity.

See page 397.

Distinguish between absorption and variable costing.

Generally accepted accounting principles require that all product costs (fixed and variable) be accumulated in inventory accounts. This practice is referred to as **absorption costing**. It is required for public reporting. However, for internal reporting many companies include only the variable product costs in the inventory accounts (frequently called **variable costing**). Fixed manufacturing costs are expensed when incurred regardless of when the inventory is sold. Under these circumstances, variable product cost acts as a proxy for relevant cost and thereby facilitates decision making. Also, variable costing discourages managers from overproducing for the purpose of delaying the expense recognition of fixed overhead costs by hiding them in inventory accounts.

Self-Study Problems

Multiple Choice Problems

1. Which of the following describes the flow of product costs through a manufacturing company?
   a. raw materials to finished goods to work in process to cost of goods sold
   b. cost of goods sold to raw materials to finished goods to work in process
   c. raw materials to work in process to finished goods to cost of goods sold
   d. work in process to raw materials to finished goods to cost of goods sold

2. The following information was drawn from the records of Common Company (CC). Beginning balance in work in process inventory was $9,000. Ending balance in work in process was $10,000. During the period, CC transferred $26,000 of raw materials to work in process. Labour costs amounted to $32,000 and overhead amounted to $33,000. Based on this information, what was the amount of cost transferred from work in process to finished goods inventory?
   a. $90,000
   b. $91,000
   c. $89,000
   d. none of the above

3. Bentley Company experienced an accounting event that affected its financial statements as indicated below:

Assets =	Liab. +	Equity	Rev. −	Exp. =	Net Inc.	Cash Flow
+ −	n/a	n/a	n/a	n/a	n/a	n/a

   Which of the following accounting events could have caused these effects on FMC's statements?
   a. Paid cash to purchased raw materials inventory
   b. Transferred cost from work in process to finished goods inventory
   c. Recognized revenue from merchandise sold for cash
   d. a and b

4. XYZ company paid cash for wages of production workers. The recognition of this event will act to:
   a. not affect assets, equity, or net income, and decrease cash flow
   b. decrease assets, equity, net income, and cash flow
   c. not affect assets, decrease net income and cash flow
   d. decrease assets, net income, and net cash flow from investing activities

5. Which of the following statements is true?
   a. The recognition of salaries paid to office workers acts to increase the work in process account.
   b. The recognition of estimated overhead cost acts to increase the work in process account.
   c. The transfer of product costs to finished goods inventory acts to decrease the amount of work in process inventory.
   d. All of the statements are true.

6. When a company recognizes amortization on manufacturing equipment:
   a. total assets increase
   b. total assets, equity, and net income decrease
   c. total assets, equity, and net income are not affected
   d. none of the above

7. Western Company purchased direct materials on account. The materials cost will be recognized as an expense when:
   a. the materials are purchased
   b. the goods made with the materials are sold
   c. the cash is paid to settle the associated accounts payable
   d. the manufacturing process is complete

8. If manufacturing overhead is underapplied, the entry to close the overhead account at the end of the accounting period will act to:
   a. increase net income
   b. decrease net income
   c. not affect net income
   d. increase cash flow from operating activities

9. The following information was drawn from the records of Y Co. Gross margin was $200, Sales were $1,400, ending finished goods inventory was $300, and cost of goods manufactured (i.e., amount transferred from work in process to finished goods) was $800. Based on this information, the beginning balance in finished goods inventory must have been:
   a. $750
   b. $800
   c. $700
   d. $850

10. At the beginning of 20X2 LMN company estimated total overhead cost to be $41,200. LMN uses direct labour hours as the allocation base for overhead costs. The company expects to use 10,000 direct labour hours during 20X2 and actually used 800 hours of direct labour in the month of January. If actual overhead costs amount to $5,000 during January, the balance in the manufacturing overhead account on January 31 would be:
   a. $1,704
   b. $5,000
   c. $ 3,296
   d. none of the above

11. In which account is the actual amount of amortization on manufacturing equipment initially recorded?
   a. Amortization Expense
   b. Work in Process Inventory
   c. Manufacturing Overhead
   d. Cost of Goods Sold

Use the following information to answer the next three questions. The XYZ Company was started on January 1, 20X1. The company incurred the following transactions during the year. (Assume all transactions are for cash unless otherwise indicated.)
   1. Issued common shares in return for $5,000 in cash from shareholders.
   2. Purchased $1,400 of direct raw materials.
   3. Used $1,000 of these direct raw materials in the production process.
   4. Paid production workers $1,800 cash.
   5. Paid $1,600 for manufacturing overhead (assume applied and actual overhead are the same).
   6. Started and completed 100 units of inventory.
   7. Sold 80 units at a price of $60 each.
   8. Paid $800 for selling and administrative expenses.

12. The amount of finished goods inventory on XYZ's balance sheet at the end of the accounting period would be:
   a. $3,520
   b. $4,000
   c. $880
   d. none of the above

13. The amount of cost of goods sold recognized by XYZ is:
   a. $3,520
   b. $4,000
   c. $880
   d. none of the above

14. The amount of net income recognized by XYZ is:
    a. $1,280
    b. $480
    c. $2,080
    d. $1,500

Use the following information to answer the next two questions: Today Company (TC) allocates overhead costs on the basis of direct labour hours. TC estimated direct labour hours to be 80,000 hours and total overhead cost to be $560,000.

15. If actual direct labour worked in February was 7,000 hours, how much overhead cost would be allocated to work in process for the month?
    a. $56,000
    b. $0
    c. $480,000
    d. $49,000

16. If actual overhead costs for the year amounted to $570,000 and actual direct labour worked amounted to 82,000 hours, then overhead would be:
    a. overapplied by $4,000
    b. underapplied by $4,000
    c. overapplied by $10,000
    d. underapplied by $10,000

Use the following information to answer the next two questions: The following beginning and ending inventory balances apply to Mendez Company (MC) 20X6 accounting period:

	Beginning	Ending
Raw Materials Inventory	$42,000	$39,000
Work in Process Inventory	$39,000	$43,000
Finished Goods Inventory	$27,000	$31,000

During 20X4, the company purchased $344,000 of direct raw materials. It incurred $290,000 of direct labour costs for the year and allocated $320,000 of manufacturing overhead costs to work in process. There was no overapplied or underapplied overhead. Revenue from goods sold during the year was $998,000

17. The amount of cost of goods manufactured (amount transferred from WIP to finished goods) was:
    a. $949,000
    b. $957,000
    c. $953,000
    d. none of the above

18. What was MC's gross margin in 20X6?
    a. $45,000
    b. $49,000
    c. $2,000
    d. None of the above.

Use the following information to answer the next two questions: Martin Manufacturing Company (MMC) produced 1,000 units of product during 20X3. The company incurred variable production cost amounting to $380 per unit. Fixed manufacturing overhead costs amounted to $130,000. MMC sold 900 units of product at a price of $800 per unit.

19. Assuming MMC uses variable costing, the amount of income recognized on the income statement would be:
    a. $248,000
    b. $210,000
    c. $261,000
    d. none of the above

20. Assuming MMC uses absorption costing, the amount of inventory shown on the balance sheet would be:
    a. $38,000
    b. $51,000
    c. $13,000
    d. none of the above

Exercise Type Problems

P1. The following trial balance was drawn from the accounting records of Lee Chong Manufacturing Company (LCMC) as of January 1, 20X1.

Cash	$52,000	
Raw Materials Inventory	6,900	
Work in Process Inventory	8,000	
Finished Goods Inventory*	7,200	
Common Shares		40,000
Retained Earnings		34,100
Totals	$74,100	$74,100

*The cost per unit of finished goods is $2.

LCMC experience the following business events during 20X1, the following transactions took place at Saint Frances Manufacturing:

1. Raw materials costing $19,000 were purchased with cash.
2. Raw materials costing $16,000 were transferred to the production department.
3. Direct labour was 2,000 hours @$9 per hour.
4. Overhead costs were applied to WIP. The predetermined overhead rate is $7 per direct labour hour.
5. Actual overhead costs amounted to $14,600 cash.
6. Work was completed on 22,000 units. The average cost per unit completed was determined to be $2 per unit.
7. 20,000 units were sold for at a price of $3 per unit.
8. Selling and administrative expenses were $11,000 paid in cash.

LCMC charges overapplied or underapplied overhead directly to cost of goods sold.

Required:
1. Open T-accounts and post the information for the 20X1 transactions including adjusting and closing entries into the T-accounts.
2. Prepare a statement of cost of goods manufactured and sold and an income statement for the 20X1 accounting period.

P1. Form for Requirement 1

Cash
Beg. 52,000
Bal. 49,400

Raw Materials
Beg. 6,900 B
Bal. 9,900

Work in Process
Beg. 8,000
Bal. 12,000

Finished Goods
Beg 7,200
Bal 11,200

Common Shares
Beg. 40,000
Bal 40,000

Retained Earnings
Beg. 34,100
Bal 42,500

Revenue

Cost of Goods Sold

Selling & Admin. Exp.

Manufacturing Overhead
Bal 0

P1. Form for Requirement 2

Lee Chong Manufacturing Company
Financial Statements for 20X1

Cost of Goods Manf. and Sold		Income Statement		Balance Sheet		Cash Flow Statement	
Beg. Raw Mat. Inv.		Sales Revenue		Assets		Oper. Activities	
Purchases		Cost of Goods Sold		Cash		Inflow from Rev.	
Raw Mat. Avail.		Gross Margin		Raw Mat. Inv.		Outflow for Inventory	
End. Raw Mat. Inv.		Sell. & Admin. Exp.		W-I-P Inv.		Outflow for Sell. & Adm.	
Raw Mat. Used		Net Income	$ 8,400	Fin. Goods Inv.		Net Inflow from Oper.	(2,600)
Direct Labour				Total Assets	$82,500	Investing Activities	
Manf. Overhead Applied						Financing Activities	
Total Manf. Costs				Equity		Net Change in Cash	
Beg. W-I-P Inv.				Common Stk.		Beg. Cash Balance	$ 49,400
Total W-I-P Inv.				Ret. Earnings		Ending Cash Balance	
End. W-I-P Inv.				Total Equity	$82,500		5
Cost of Goods Man.							
Beg. Fin. Goods							
Goods Available for Sale							
End. Fin. Goods							
Cost of Goods Sold - Unadjusted							
Plus: Underapplied Overhead							
Cost of Goods Sold - Adjusted	$40,600						

P2. Dunn Company incurred the following costs during its most recent accounting period.

Manufacturing Costs
- Variable — $40 per unit
- Fixed — $20,000 total

Selling and Administrative Expenses
- Variable — $16 per unit
- Fixed — $14,000 total

Dunn produced 2,000 units and sold 1,850 units at a price of $95 per unit.

Required:
1. Prepare an income statement under absorption costing.
2. Prepare an income statement under variable costing.
3. Explain why managers may be motivated to use absorption costing as opposed to variable costing.

P2. Form for Requirement 1

Dunn Company Income Statement (Absorption Costing)	
Net Income	$39,650

P2. Form for Requirement 2

Dunn Company Income Statement (Variable Costing)	
Net Income	$ 38,150

P2. Form for Requirement 3

Multiple Choice Problems - Solutions

1. c

2. a   Beg. WIP + Raw Materials + Labour + Overhead − Transferred Out = End WIP
   $9,000 + $26,000 + $32,000 + $33,000 − X = $10,000
   − X = $10,000 − $9,000 − $26,000 − $32,000 − $33,000
   X = $90,000

3. d

4. a

5. d

6. c

7. b

8. b

9. c   Revenue − Cost of Goods Sold = Gross Margin
   Cost of Goods Sold = Revenue − Gross Margin
   Cost of Goods Sold = $1,400 − $200 = $1,200
   Accordingly, we conclude that $1,200 was transferred from finished goods inventory to cost of goods sold.

   Beg. Finished Goods + Cost of Goods Manufactured − Cost of Goods Sold = End Finished Goods
   Beg. Finished Goods = End Finished Goods − Cost of Goods Manufactured + Cost of Goods Sold
   Beg. Finished Goods = $300 − $800 + 1,200 = $700

10. a   Predetermined OH Rate = Total Estimated OH Cost ÷ Allocation Base
    Predetermined OH Rate = $41,200 ÷ 10,000 Labour Hours = $4.12 Per Labour Hour

    Amount of OH Applied During Period = $4.12 x 800 hours = $3,296
    Since the amount of actual overhead ($5,000) acts to increase the MOH account and the amount of applied overhead ($3,296) acts to decrease the MOH account, the balance in the account would be $1,704 ($5,000 − $3,296).

11. c

12. c   The cost of the 100 units that were finished was $4,400 ($1,000 materials + $1,800 labour + $1,600 overhead). Cost per unit was $44 ($4,400 ÷ 100 units). The cost of goods sold was $3,520 ($44 per unit x 80 units). The ending finished goods inventory was $880 ($4,400 cost of finished goods − $3,520 cost of goods sold).

13. a   See computation in solution to question number 12.

14. b   Revenue − Cost of Goods Sold − S&A Expense = Net Income
    $4,800 − $3,520 − $800 = $480

15. d   Overhead Rate = Total Expected OH Cost ÷ Allocation Base
    Overhead Rate = $560,000 ÷ 80,000 Hours = $7 Per Hour
    $7 Per Hour x 7,000 Hours = $49,000 Allocated Overhead for the Month of February.

16. a Overhead Applied for the year would have been $574,000 (82,000 Hours x $7 Per Hour). Since applied overhead ($574,000) is over the amount of the actual overhead cost ($570,000), the overhead is said to be overapplied by the $4,000 difference ($574,000 – $570,000).

17. c See schedule below:

Mendez Company
Cost of Goods Manufactured and Sold
For Period Ended 12/31/20X6

Beginning Raw Materials Inventory	$ 42,000
Plus Purchases	344,000
Raw Materials Available for Use	386,000
Less Ending Raw Materials Inventory	(39,000)
Direct Raw Materials Used	347,000
Direct Labour	290,000
Overhead Cost Applied	320,000
Total Manufacturing Costs	957,000
Plus Beginning Work in process Inventory	39,000
Total Work in process Inventory	996,000
Less Ending Work in process Inventory	(43,000)
Cost of Goods Manufactured	953,000
Plus Beginning Finished Goods Inventory	27,000
Cost of Goods Available for Sale	980,000
Less Ending Finished Goods Inventory	(31,000)
Cost of Goods Sold	949,000

18. b See schedule shown in solution to question 17 for the computation of the amount of cost of goods sold.

Revenue – Cost of Goods Sold = Gross Margin
$998,000 – $949,000 = $49,000

19. a
Revenue (900 Units x $800)	$720,000
Variable Cost (900 Units x $380)	(342,000)
Fixed Cost	(130,000)
Income	$248,000

20. b Cost Per Unit [($380 x 1,000 Units) + $130,000] ÷ 1,000 Units = $510
Ending Inventory Balance 100 Units x $510 = $51,000

Exercise Type Problems - Solutions

P1. Solution for Requirements 1

Cash

Beg.	52,000	(1)	19,000
(7)	60,000	(3)	18,000
		(5)	14,600
		(8)	11,000
Bal.	49,400		

Raw Materials

Beg.	6,900	(2)	16,000
(1)	19,000		
Bal.	9,900		

Work in Process

Beg.	8,000	(6)	44,000
(2)	16,000		
(3)	18,000		
(4)	14,000		
Bal.	12,000		

Finished Goods

Beg.	7,200	(7)	40,000
(6)	44,000		
Bal.	11,200		

Manufacturing Overhead

(5)	14,600	(4)	14,000
		(adj)	600
Bal	0		

Common Shares

		Beg.	40,000
		Bal	40,000

Retained Earnings

		Beg.	34,100
(cl)	8,400		
		Bal	42,500

Revenue

(cl)	60,000	(7)	60,000

Cost of Goods Sold

(7)	40,000	(cl)	40,600
adj	600		

Selling & Admin. Exp.

(8)	11,000	(cl)	11,000

197

P1. Form for Requirement 2

Lee Chong Manufacturing Company
Financial Statements for 20X1

Cost of Goods Manf. and Sold

Beg. Raw Mat. Inv.	$ 6,900
Purchases	19,000
Raw Mat. Avail.	25,900
End. Raw Mat. Inv.	(9,900)
Raw Mat. Used	16,000
Direct Labour	18,000
Manf. Overhead Applied	14,000
Total Manf. Costs	48,000
Beg. W-I-P Inv.	8,000
Total W-I-P Inv.	56,000
End. W-I-P Inv.	(12,000)
Cost of Goods Man.	44,000
Beg. Fin. Goods	7,200
Goods Available for Sale	51,200
End. Fin. Goods	(11,200)
Cost of Goods Sold Unadjusted	$40,000
Plus: Underapplied Overhead	600
Cost of Goods Sold Adjusted	$40,600

[1]$19,000 + $18,000 + $14,600 = $51,600 (Event Nos. 1, 3, and 5)

Income Statement

Sales Revenue	$ 60,000
Cost of Goods Sold	(40,600)
Gross Margin	19,400
Sell. & Admin. Exp.	(11,000)
Net Income	$ 8,400

Balance Sheet

Assets		
Cash	$ 49,400	
Raw Mat. Inv.	9,900	
W-I-P Inv.	12,000	
Fin. Goods Inv.	11,200	
Total Assets		$82,500
Equity		
Common Stk.	$40,000	
Ret. Earnings	42,500	
Total Equity		$82,500

Cash Flow Statement

Oper. Activities		
Inflow from Rev.	$60,000	
Outflow for Inventory[1]	(51,600)	
Outflow for Sell. & Adm.	(11,000)	
Net Inflow from Oper.		(2,600)
Investing Activities		0
Financing Activities		0
Net Change in Cash		(2,600)
Beg. Cash Balance		52,000
Ending Cash Balance		$ 49,400

5

P2. Solution for Requirement 1

Dunn Company Income Statement (Absorption Costing)	
Revenues ($95 x 1,850 units)	$175,750
C. of G. Sold ($50* x 1,850 units)	(92,500)
Gross Margin	83,250
Variable S&A Expenses ($16 x 1,850 units)	(29,600)
Fixed S&A Expenses	(14,000)
Net Income	$39,650

*Product Cost Per Unit: [($40 x 2,000) + $20,000] ÷ 2,000 = $50

P2. Solution for Requirement 2

Dunn Company Income Statement (Variable Costing)	
Revenues ($95 x 1,850 units)	$175,750
Variable Costs	
Manufacturing ($40 x 1,850 units)	(74,000)
S&A Expense ($16 x 1,850 units)	(29,600)
Contribution Margin	72,150
Fixed costs	
Manufacturing	(20,000)
S&A Expenses	(14,000)
Net Income	$ 38,150

P2. Solution for Requirement 3

As indicated by the above statements, absorption costing enables managers to produce favorable financial statements by producing more inventory than is sold. This is so because fixed manufacturing costs are accumulated in the inventory account. Presenting favorable financial statements may be advantageous in obtaining financing and in elevating bonuses that are based on performance as measured by net income.

Chapter 12
Job-Order, Process, And Hybrid Cost Systems

Learning Objectives for the Chapter

The material in this chapter of the study guide, is designed to facilitate your ability to:

- Distinguish between job-order and process cost systems.
- Identify product cost flows through a job-order cost system.
- Identify product cost flows through a process cost system.
- Distinguish between raw materials cost and transfer-in cost.
- Understand how hybrid accounting systems can be created by combining different components of job-order and process cost systems.
- Identify the various forms of documentation used in a job-order cost system.
- Understand how accounting events in a job-order system affect financial statements.
- Understand how accounting events in a process cost system affect financial statements.
- Convert partially complete units into equivalent whole units.

Brief Explanation of the Learning Objectives

Distinguish between job-order and process cost systems.

Cost accounting systems designed to accumulate costs by individual products or batches of products are called **job-order** cost systems. For example, if your were building houses you would likely use a job-order system so that you could determine the cost of each particular house that you build. In contrast, cost systems designed to distribute costs evenly over a homogeneous product line are called **process** cost systems. A process cost system would be used to determine the average cost of making a can of soda, or a gallon of paint, or a pair of shoes, etc. In summary, job-order systems are used to account for the individual cost of heterogeneous products, while process cost systems are used to determine the average unit cost of making a number of the exact same product.

Identify product cost flows through a job-order cost system.

In a **job order system**, total product costs flow through raw materials inventory to work in process inventory to finished goods inventory and out to cost of goods sold. Detailed information about each individual inventory item is maintained in subsidiary documents known as a **job order cost sheets**. For example, suppose a company incurs $10,000 of labour cost, 40% of which is used on job no. 101 and 60% of which is used on job no.

102. In this case $10,000 would be transferred to the work in process control account. Also, $4,000 ($10,000 x .4) would be added to the job cost sheet of job 101 and $6,000 would be added to the job cost sheet of job 102. Since the same cost data is placed in the inventory control account, and the subsidiary cost sheets, the total of the work in process control account ($10,000) must reconcile with (i.e., be the same) the total of the amounts show in the cost sheets ($4,000 + $6,000).

Identify product cost flows through a process cost system.

In a **process cost system**, total product costs flow from raw materials inventory through a *series of departmental* work in process inventory accounts to finished goods inventory and out to cost of goods sold. Since all units of a product are the same, the unit cost is determined by dividing the total cost of processing the products by the total number of products made. Accordingly, unit cost is measured as an average rather than an actual amount.

Distinguish between raw materials cost and transfer-in cost.

In process cost systems, accumulated product costs are passed from one department to the next. The cost of products completed in one department include the raw materials, labour, and overhead incurred by that department. When these accumulated costs are passed on to the next department, they are called *transfer-in costs*. For example, the cutting department of a furniture manufacturer may transfer wooden table legs to an assembly department. The cost of these legs would be called a transfer-in cost of the assembly department. The assembly department may add raw materials (e.g., glass tops) to the table legs in the process of assembling the tables. In this case, the costs incurred by the assembly department would include the transfer-in cost of the table legs, the raw materials cost of the glass tops, labour costs, and overhead.

Understand how hybrid accounting systems can be created by combining different components of job-order and process cost systems.

Hybrid cost systems blend some of the features of a job-order costing system with some of the features of a process cost system. For example, Gateway 2000 makes hundreds of thousands of computers with standard features. These computers are produced through a continuous flow assembly line process that is compatible with process costing. Each unit requires the same amount of labour to assemble the same standard set of parts into finished products (i.e., computers) that are ready-made for immediate delivery. However, Gateway also accepts customer orders for customized products that have unique features. For example, some customers may want a larger monitor, more memory, or a faster processor than comes with a designated standard model. Gateway will accommodate these requests by customizing the products as they move through the production process. The customized features will require cost tracing features that are commonly associated with job-order costing. Accordingly, Gateway will use a hybrid costing system that combines some of the features of both process and job-order costing.

Identify the various forms of documentation used in a job-order cost system.

In a job-order cost system product costs are accumulated on a document known as a job cost sheet. There are two primary source documents for the information that is recorded on the job cost sheet. The first is called a **materials requisition form**. The information regarding material requisitions for each job is communicated to the accounting department where it is summarized on the job cost sheet. The second source document for the job cost sheet is a *work ticket*, sometimes called a time card. The work ticket includes space for the job number, employee identification, and work description. The amount of time spent on each job is recorded on the work ticket. The work tickets are forwarded to the accounting department where the wage rates are recorded and the amount of labour cost is computed for each job and recorded on the job cost sheet. Finally, each job cost sheet provides space for the inclusion of the amount of applied overhead. The job cost sheets are maintained perpetually with new cost data being added as work on the job progresses. Accordingly, a prorated share of the estimated overhead cost will be systematically added to each job cost sheet through the use of a predetermined overhead rate.

Understand how accounting events in a job-order system affect financial statements.

You should be able to record accounting events in a financial statements model like the one shown below. You should be able to record the events regardless of whether a company uses a job-order or process cost system.

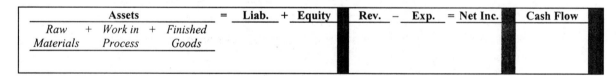

Convert partially complete units into equivalent whole units.

Ending work in process inventory is normally composed of units of product that are only partially complete. These partially complete units must be converted to equivalent whole units in order to determine the average cost per unit of product. The logic employed to convert partial units to equivalent whole units uses simple mathematics. For example, two units that are 50% complete are equal to one equivalent whole unit (i.e., 2 x .5 = 1). Similarly, four units that are 25% complete are equal to one equivalent whole unit (i.e., 4 x .25 = 1). Likewise, 100 units that are 30% complete are equal to 30 equivalent whole units (i.e., 100 units x .30).

Multiple Choice Problems

1. Which of the following businesses is most likely to use a job order cost system?
   a. a hospital
   b. an auto manufacturing company
   c. a paint manufacturer
   d. a bank

2. The cost of goods transferred from one department to another is called:
   a. transportation cost
   b. transfer-in cost
   c. finished goods cost
   d. none of the above

3. RST's accountant made the following entry into the accounting records:

Work in Process Assembly Department	xxx	
Work in Process Cutting Department		xxx

   Which of the following describes the effect of this entry on the accounting equation?
   a. Total assets and total liabilities increase.
   b. Total assets are unaffected, but total equity increases.
   c. Total assets and total equity are unaffected.
   d. Total assets decrease and total liabilities increase.

4. KLM Company paid cash wages to production workers. Which of the following choices correctly describes how this event will affect the company's financial statements?
   a. Total assets will increase if the company uses a job-order system, but will decrease if the company uses a process cost system.
   b. Total assets will not be affected regardless if the company uses a job-order system or a process cost system.
   c. Total equity will increase if the company uses a process cost system but will decrease if it uses a job order system.
   d. a and c.

5. AST Electronics installs TV satellite dishes. The company is currently working on two jobs. The job order cost sheets for Job 505 and Job 506 provide the following information:

	Job 505	Job 506
Direct Materials	$60	$50
Direct Labour	$100	$80

ABC applies overhead jobs at $.70 per direct labour dollar. Job 506 is finished and has been sold for $300. ABC's gross margin on Job 506 is:
a. $300
b. $130
c. $186
d. $114

Use the following information to answer the next two questions. The following information was drawn from the accounting records of Glide Manufacturing Company (GMC). As the data suggest, GMC uses a job-order costing system:

	Job 101	Job 102	Job 103
Direct Materials	$3,500	$4,200	$3,300
Direct Labour	$2,800	$3,600	$1,900

The predetermined overhead rate is set at 120% of direct labour costs. At the end of the accounting period, Jobs 101 and 102 had been completed and sold. Job 103 was still under construction.

6. The balance in the work in process inventory is
   a. $7,480
   b. $5,200
   c. $7,100
   d. None of the above.

7. Determine the gross margin recognized on Job 102 assuming it is sold for $18,000. Ignore any overapplied or underapplied overhead.)
   a. $250
   b. $50
   c. $150
   d. none of the above

Use the following information to answer the next two questions. The Rock Wall Company makes stone retainer walls for commercial and residential properties. The company had two walls under construction during the month of February. The data apply to these two jobs.

	Job 40	Job 41
Direct Materials	$12,000	$24,000
Direct Labour	$26,000	$36,000

At the beginning of the year Rock Wall's accountant estimated that the total annual overhead cost would amount to $360,000 and that the annual direct labour cost would amount to $500,000.

8. The amount of overhead applied to the work in process account during the month of February is
   a. $25,920
   b. $62,000
   c. $44,640
   d. none of the above

9. If actual annual labour cost amount to $520,000 and actual annual overhead costs $370,000, overhead will be:
   a. overapplied by $10,000
   b. overapplied by $4,400
   c. underapplied by $4,400
   d. underapplied by $10,000

10. Which of the following companies is most likely to use a process cost system?
    a. Ship Building
    b. Home Construction
    c. Swimming Pool Construction.
    d. Soft Drink Bottling

11. Garrett Software Systems (GSS) uses a process cost system. The following data applies to the company's most recent accounting period. GSS started the accounting period with 5,000 units of product in beginning inventory. The company started work on 60,000 units of product during the period. At the end of the period there were 4,000 units of product in work in process inventory. These units were estimated to be 60% complete. Based on this information, the total number of equivalent units (units completed plus units in ending inventory) is
    a. 63,400
    b. 65,000
    c. 69,000
    d. 61,000

Use the following information to answer the next two questions: A review of Burkowski Manufacturing Company's (BMC) work in process inventory account indicated the following activity measured in units.

Beginning Inventory	8,000
Started	56,000
Ending Inventory	6,000

The ending inventory was estimated to be 80% complete. Product cost in the work in process account at the beginning of the period amounted to $48,000. There was $517,200 of product cost added to the work in process account during the period.

12. What is the number of equivalent units in Burkowski's ending work in process inventory?
    a. 6,000
    b. 1,200
    c. 4,800
    d. none of the above

13. The amount of cost in ending work-in-process inventory is
    a. $72,000
    b. $54,000
    c. $62,800
    d. $43,200

14. Twin County Rockers (TCR) makes rocking chairs. The chairs are processed through two departments. Raw lumber is placed into the cutting department where it is made into chair parts. The chair parts are transferred to the assembly department where the chairs are put together. The transfer-in cost for the assembly department would include:
    a. the cost of raw lumber
    b. the cost of labour and overhead incurred in the cutting department
    c. the cost of overhead incurred in the assembly department
    d. a and b

Exercise Type Problems

P1. Bailey's Boat Dock Company (BBDC) is owned and operated by Bill Bailey. Bill operates the company as a part time business that supplements his day job income. BBDC normally produces three or four boat docks per year. BBC started the company with no beginning inventory. Three boat docks were started during the accounting period. The costs incurred for each job are shown below:

Special Orders	Materials	Labour
Job 401	$4,900	$2,300
Job 402	8,200	5,400
Job 403	5,300	3,100

Overhead is applied to each job at the rate of 40% of direct labour dollars. Actual overhead costs incurred during the accounting period amounted $4,500. Construction on Jobs 401 and 403 was completed during the period. Job 401 was sold for $10,500. Negotiations for the sale of Job 403 were underway but the dock had not been sold by the end of the accounting period. Job 402 was a large project that remained under construction at end of the accounting period.

Required:

1. Compute the balances that would appear in the inventory accounts shown on the year-end balance sheet.
2. Determine the amount of underapplied or overapplied overhead for the year.
3. Determine the gross margin that would appear on the year-end income statement. Assume that any underapplied or overapplied overhead is considered insignificant.

P1. Form for Requirement 1

Job Number	Materials	Labour	Overhead	Total

P1. Form for Requirement 2

P1. Form for Requirement 3

Job Number	Materials	Labour	Overhead	Total

P2. The Leather Case Manufacturing Company makes and sells leather briefcases. Leather hides are distributed to the cutting department, which cuts the hides into pieces of leather. The leather pieces are then sent to a sewing department where they are sewn together to form brief cases. The brief cases are then sent to the finishing department where hinges, buckles, snaps, etc. are attached to the cases. The sewing department's work-in-process account had a $42,000 balance as of October 1st. During the month of October the sewing department received $175,600 of parts from the cutting department. Labour cost incurred by the sewing department amounted to $263,000. Finally, there was $315,600 of overhead that was applied to the sewing department during October. The volume of production (measured in number of units) for the sewing department during the month of October is shown below.

Beginning Inventory	700
Started	11,000
Units Completed	10,900

The ending inventory in the sewing department is estimated to be 80% complete.

Required:

1. Determine the total number of equivalent units produced by the sewing department in October (units completed plus units in ending inventory).
2. Determine the cost per equivalent unit for briefcases made in the sewing department.
3. Determine the cost of inventory transferred from the sewing department to the finishing department and the cost of the ending work in process in the sewing department's work in process account.

P2. Form for Requirement 1

Units in Ending Inventory	800

Total Equivalent Units	11,540

P2. Form for Requirement 2

P2. Form for Requirement 3

Multiple Choice Problems - Solutions

1. a

2. b

3. c

4. b One asset account (cash) will decrease and another asset account (work in process) will increase regardless of whether the company uses a job-order or a process cost system.

5. d The cost of job 506 is $186 [$50 + $80 + ($80 x $0.70)]. The gross margin is $114 ($300 – $186).

6. a The cost of job 103 is $7,480 [$3,300 + $1,900 + ($1,900 x 1.2)].

7. d The cost of job 102 is $12,120 [$4,200 + $3,600 + ($3,600 x 1.2)]. The gross margin is $5,880 ($18,000 – $12,120).

8. c Predetermined Overhead Rate = $360,000 + $500,000 = $0.72 Per Labour Dollar
Applied Overhead = [$0.72 x ($26,000 + $36,000)] = $44,640

9. b Applied Overhead = $520,000 x $0.72 = $374,400
Since the actual overhead ($370,000) is less than the applied overhead the overhead is classified as being overapplied. The amount of the over application is $4,400 ($374,400 – $370,000).

10. d

11. a

Beginning Inventory	5,000
Started	60,000
Available	65,000
Less Ending Inventory	(4,000)
Units Completed	61,000
Plus Equivalent Units in Ending Inventory*	2,400
Total Equivalent Units	63,400

*4,000 Units x .6 = 2,400 Units

12. c 6,000 Units x .8 = 4,800 units

13. d

Beginning Inventory	8,000
Started	56,000
Available	64,000
Less Ending Inventory	(6,000)
Units Completed	58,000
Plus Equivalent Units in Ending Inventory*	4,800
Total Equivalent Units	62,800

*6,000 Units x .8 = 4,800 units

Cost Per Equivalent Unit = ($48,000 + $517,200) + 62,800 Units = $9
Cost in Ending Inventory = 4,800 Equivalent Units x $9 = 43,200

14. d Transfer-in cost of the assembly department would include the cost of materials, labour, and overhead incurred by the cutting department.

Exercise Type Problems - Solutions

P1. Solution for Requirement 1

There are two inventory accounts that would appear on the balance sheet. Job 402 is a work in process account and Job 403 is a finished goods account. The cost of the two jobs is shown below.

Job Number	Materials	Labour	Overhead	Total	
Job 402	$8,200	$5,400	$2,160*	$15,760	WIP Inventory
Job 403	$5,300	$3,100	$1,240*	$ 9,640	Finished Goods Inv.

*$5,400 x .4 = $2,160
*$3,100 x .4 = $1,240

P1. Solution for Requirement 2

The amount of applied overhead is $4,320 [($2,300 + $5,400 + $3,100) x .4]. Since the amount of applied overhead is less than the actual overhead ($4,500), the overhead is underapplied. The amount of the underapplication is $180 ($4,320 − $4,500).

P1. Solution for Requirement 3

The cost of Job 401 is shown below.

Job Number	Materials	Labour	Overhead	Total	
Job 401	$4,900	$2,300	$920*	$8,120	WIP Inventory

*$2,300 x .4 = $920

The amount of cost of goods sold is the cost of Job 401 plus the amount of the underapplied overhead, the total of which is $8,300 ($8,120 + $180).

The gross margin is $2,200 ($10,500 − $8,300).

P2. Solution for Requirement 1

Beginning Inventory	700
Started	11,000
Available	11,700
Less Units Completed	(10,900)
Units in Ending Inventory	800
Equivalent Units in Ending Inventory*	640
Units Completed	10,900
Total Equivalent Units	11,540

*800 Units x .8 = 640 Units

P2. Solution for Requirement 2

Cost Per Equivalent Unit is $69 [($42,000 + $175,600 + $263,000 + $315,600) + 11,540].

P2. Solution for Requirement 3

The cost transferred to the finishing department is $752,100 (10,900 Units x $69).
The cost of ending WIP in the sewing department is $44,160 (640 Units x $69).

Chapter 13
Financial Statement Analysis

Learning Objectives for the Chapter

The material in this chapter of the study guide is designed to facilitate your ability to:

- Describe the factors associated with the communication of useful information.
- Differentiate between horizontal and vertical analysis.
- Understand what the term *ratio analysis* means.
- Calculate the ratios that facilitate the assessment of a company's debt paying ability.
- Calculate the ratios that facilitate the assessment of a company's solvency.
- Calculate the ratios that facilitate the assessment of a company's managerial effectiveness.
- Calculate the ratios that facilitate the assessment of a company's position in the stock market.
- Identify different forms for presenting analytical data.
- Understand the limitations of financial statement analysis.

Brief Explanation of the Learning Objectives

Describe the factors associated with the communication of useful information.

When trying to determine what information should be communicated to users, and in what form the information should be communicated, accountants consider several factors. Factors to be considered include:
- The nature of the decisions being made.
- The sophistication of the user with respect to their understanding of financial information.
- The need to make the information as easy and as efficient to use as possible.
- The desire to avoid information overload. That is, the desire to avoid providing a lot of data that the user does not need to make his or her decision.

Differentiate between horizontal and vertical analysis.

Horizontal analysis involves comparing similar data related to the same company from several accounting periods. The data compared can be in absolute terms or in percentage terms, but comparing absolute amounts over time requires special caution if the user is not to be misled.

Vertical analysis involves converting the financial statements into percentage terms. For the income statement, all items are usually restated as a percentage of net sales, so net sales is equal to 100%. For the balance sheet all items are restated as a percentage of total assets.

Financial statements that are restated into a percentage format are sometimes referred to as "common sized financial statements."

Understand what the term *ratio analysis* means.

For decision making purposes, it is usually easier to consider data that are presented in relative terms rather than absolute terms. This is the motivation behind vertical analysis, but ratios can be computed without converting the entire financial statement into percentage terms. Furthermore, ratios are often computed that do not appear on percentage based financial statements. Simply stated, ratio analysis always involves dividing one item of numerical business datum by another item of business datum.

Calculate the ratios that facilitate the assessment of a company's debt paying ability.

This chapter included discussion of eleven different ratios that might be used to help assess a company's debt paying ability. Seven of these relate to liquidity, the ability to pay debts in the short-term, and five relate to solvency, the ability to pay debts in the long-term. The liquidity ratios are:

Ratio	Formula
Current ratio	Current assets ÷ Current liabilities
Quick ratio	(Current assets – (inventory and prepaids)) ÷ Current liabilities
Accounts receivable turnover	Net credit sales ÷ Average net receivables
Average collection period	365 ÷ Accounts receivable turnover
Inventory turnover	Cost of goods sold ÷ Average inventory
Days to sell inventory	365 ÷ Inventory turnover

Calculate the ratios that facilitate the assessment of a company's solvency.

There are five ratios discussed in this chapter that relate to assessing a company's solvency. These ratios are:

Ratio	Formula
Liabilities to total equity	Total liabilities ÷ Total equity (same as total assets)
Shareholders' equity ratio	Shareholders' equity ÷ Total equity (same as total assets)
Debt-to-equity ratio	Total debt ÷ Shareholders' equity
Times bond interest earned	Income before bond interest and taxes ÷ Bond interest
Plant assets to long-term liabilities	Net plant assets ÷ Long-term liabilities

Calculate the ratios that facilitate the assessment of a company's managerial effectiveness.

There are five ratios discussed in this chapter that help assess management's ability to utilize a company's resources to efficiently produce a profit. These ratios are:

Ratio	Formula
Net margin (return on sales)	Net income ÷ Net sales
Turnover of assets	Net sales ÷ Total assets
Return-on-investment (return on assets)	Net income ÷ Total assets
Return-on-equity	Net income ÷ Shareholders' equity

Calculate ratios that facilitate the assessment of a company's position in stock market.

There are four ratios discussed in this chapter that help assess a company's position in the stock market. These ratios are:

Ratio	Formula
Earnings per share (EPS)	Net earnings available for common shareholders' ÷ Average number of shares of common stock outstanding
Book value per share	(Shareholders' equity − preferred shareholders' rights) ÷ Average number of shares of common stock outstanding
Price-to-earnings ratio (P/E)	Market price per share ÷ Earnings per share
Dividend yield	Dividends per share ÷ Market price per share

Identify different forms for presenting analytical data.

In addition to being reported in ratio form, analytical data are often presented in charts and graphs. A graphical format is often used in companies' annual reports to present information that is not required by a regulating body (e.g. Québec Securities Commission) or by generally accepted accounting principles.

Understand the limitations of financial statement analysis.

There are many factors that make financial statement analysis difficult. These include the difficulty of:
- comparing companies in different industries.
- comparing companies that use different accounting estimates and methods.
- comparing a company's current results to prior periods' results when major changes have occurred, such as a merger or a major change in the economy..

Self-Study Problems
Multiple-Choice Problems

1. Which of the following statements about financial statement analysis is true?
    a. The *book value per share* is a profitability ratio.
    b. The *debt-to-equity ratio* is a solvency ratio.
    c. The *return-on-equity* is a liquidity ratio.
    d. The *quick ratio* is a stock market ratio.

2. Which of the following statements about ratio analysis is <u>false</u>?
    a. A company prefers to have its *price-to-earnings ratio* be lower rather than higher.
    b. A company prefers to have its *inventory turnover ratio* be higher rather than lower.
    c. A company trying to increase its creditworthiness prefers to have its *debt-to-equity ratio* be lower rather than higher.
    d. A company prefers to have its *net margin* be higher rather than lower.

3. Which of the following statements about financial statement analysis is true?
    a. *Working capital* is defined as: current assets - (inventory + prepaid assets).
    b. *Vertical analysis* refers to comparing different companies in the same industry.
    c. In order to conduct a *horizontal analysis*, a company's financial data must be converted from an absolute format to a percentage format.
    d. In order to perform *trend analysis*, financial data from more than one accounting period must be obtained.

The Following Information Pertains to the Next Four Questions:

Big Truck Company
Balance Sheet as of December 13, 20X5

Current Assets:			Current liabilities:	
Cash	$ 10,000		Accounts payable	$150,000
Accounts receivable	90,000		Taxes payable	20,000
Inventory	135,000		Interest payable	10,000
Prepaid insurance	15,000			180,000
	250,000		Long-term Liabilities:	
Long-term Assets:			Notes payable	50,000
Equipment	150,000		Bonds payable	250,000
Buildings	250,000			300,000
Land	50,000		Total liabilities	480,000
Goodwill	50,000			
	500,000		Shareholders' Equity:	
Total assets	$750,000		Common stock	100,000
			Retained earnings	170,000
			Total Shareholders' Equity	
				270,000
			Total liabilities & Shareholders' Equity	$750,000

4. What is the amount of Big Truck's working capital?
   a. $270,000
   b. $250,000
   c. $100,000
   d. $ 70,000

5. What is Big Truck's *debt-to-equity* ratio?
   a. 1.11 to 1.0
   b. 1.78 to 1.0
   c. .64 to 1.0
   d. .72 to 1.0

6. What is Big Truck's *current* ratio?
   a. 1.39 to 1.0
   b. 1.80 to 1.0
   c. .56 to 1.0
   d. .72 to 1.0

7. What is Big Truck's *quick* ratio?
   a. 1.39 to 1.0
   b. 1.80 to 1.0
   c. .56 to 1.0
   d. .72 to 1.0

The Following Information Pertains to the Next Six Questions:

Information from the Balance Sheet of Bell Mesa Company:

	20X2	20X1
Cash	$ 10,000	$ 11,000
Accounts receivable	98,000	92,000
Inventory	155,000	164,000
Property plant & equipment	737,000	667,000
Total assets	$1,000,000	$934,000
Accounts payable	$ 96,500	$ 98,500
Interest payable	3,500	3,500
Bonds payable	600,000	600,000
Total liabilities	700,000	702,000
Common stock (10,000 shares outstanding)	100,000	100,000
Retained earnings	200,000	132,000
Total shareholders' equity	300,000	232,000
Total liabilities & shareholders' equity	$1,000,000	$934,000

Information from the Income Statement of Bell Mesa Company:

Sales	$ 850,000
Cost of goods sold	(537,500)
Selling and administrative expenses	(157,000)
Interest expense (on bonds)	(42,000)
Income tax expense	(45,000)
Net income	$ 68,000

8. What is Bell Mesa's *days to collect accounts receivable* ratio?
    a. 41 days
    b. 65 days
    c. 68 days
    d. 108 days

9. What is Bell Mesa's *days to sell inventory* ratio?
    a. 41 days
    b. 65 days
    c. 68 days
    d. 108 days

10. What is Bell Mesa's *times bond interest earned* ratio?
    a. 1.62 times
    b. 2.62 times
    c. 3.69 times
    d. 20.24 times

11. What is Bell Mesa's *net margin percentage*?
    a. 36.8%
    b. 18.2%
    c. 8.0%
    d. 6.8%

12. What is Bell Mesa's *book value per share* for 20X2?
    a. $ 10
    b. $ 30
    c. $ 70
    d. $100

13. What is Bell Mesa's *return on investment*?
    a. 6.8%
    b. 8.0%
    c. 22.7%
    d. 85.0%

The Following Information Pertains to the Next Three Questions:

The following information is available for the Buckcreek Stone Company for 20X9:

Net earnings	$214,000
Average number of shares of Common Stock outstanding (The common stock has no par value.)	100,000
Average number of shares of Preferred Stock outstanding (Par value = $100, dividend rate = 7%)	2,000
Market price per share of Common Stock	$ 37.00
Market price per share of Preferred Stock	$ 105.00
Dividend per share paid on Common Stock	$ 0.75

14. What is Buckcreek's *earnings per share*?
    a. $1.25
    b. $2.00
    c. $2.07
    d. $2.10

15. What is Buckcreek's *dividend yield* on Common Stock?
    a. 37.5%
    b. 2.0%
    c. 7.0%
    d. 35.0%

16. ASSUMING Buckcreek's earnings per share is $3.00, what is its *price/earnings* ratio?
    a. 12.3
    b. 5.8
    c. 4.0
    d. a negative number

Exercise Type Problems

P1. The following income statements and balance sheets are provided for Fireplace Products, Inc.

Income Statements
(amounts in thousands)

	20X5	20X4
Net sales	$6,000	$5,000
Cost of goods sold	4,740	3,900
Gross margin	1,260	1,100
Selling and administrative expenses	570	450
Operating income	690	650
Income tax expense	252	247
Net income	$ 438	$ 403

(Continued on next page.)

P1. continued

Balance Sheets
(amounts in thousands)

	20X5	20X4
ASSETS		
Current assets:		
Cash	$ 301	$ 507
Accounts receivable, net	1,055	850
Inventory	1,663	1,356
Total current assets	3,019	2,713
Property, plant, and equipment, net	1,444	997
Intangible assets, net	37	40
Total assets	$4,500	$3,750
LIABILITIES AND SHAREHOLDERS' EQUITY		
Current liabilities:		
Accounts payable	$1,315	$1,024
Accrued liabilities	647	592
Taxes payable	84	79
Total current liabilities	2,046	1,695
Notes payable	54	55
Bonds payable	600	450
Total liabilities	2,700	2,200
Shareholders' equity:		
Common stock (no-par, 13 shares outstanding)	307	307
Retained earnings	1,493	1,243
Total shareholders' equity	1,800	1,550
Total liabilities and shareholders' equity	$4,500	$3,750

Required:

Using the forms provided below, prepare vertical analysis income statements and balance sheets for Fireplace Products, Inc. Round the percentages to one decimal place.

P1. Forms for Vertical Analysis

Income Statements

	20X5	20X4
Net sales	%	%
Cost of goods sold	_____	
Gross margin		
Selling and administrative expenses	_____	
Operating income		
Income tax expense	_____	
Net income	%	%

Balance Sheets

	20X5	20X4
ASSETS		
Current assets:		
Cash	%	%
Accounts receivable, net		
Inventory	_____	
Total current assets		
Property, plant, and equipment, net		
Intangible assets, net	_____	
Total assets	%	%
LIABILITIES AND SHAREHOLDERS' EQUITY		
Current liabilities:		
Accounts payable	%	%
Accrued liabilities		
Taxes payable	_____	
Total current liabilities		
Notes payable		
Bonds payable	_____	
Total liabilities	_____	
Shareholders' equity:		
Common stock		
(no-par, 13 shares outstanding)		
Retained earnings	_____	
Total shareholders' equity	_____	
Total liabilities and shareholders' equity	%	%

P2. The following financial statements are provided for Smith's Specialty Stores.

Income Statement

	20X7
Net sales	$800,000
Cost of goods sold	536,500
Gross margin	263,500
Selling and administrative expenses	97,500
Operating income	166,000
Income tax expense	114,400
Net income	$ 51,600

Balance Sheet

		20X7
ASSETS		
Current assets:		
Cash	$ 40,500	
Accounts receivable, net	70,000	
Inventory	91,000	
Total current assets		$201,500
Property, plant, and equipment, net		320,500
Intangible assets, net		88,000
Total assets		$610,000
LIABILITIES AND SHAREHOLDERS' EQUITY		
Current liabilities:		
Accounts payable	$103,500	
Accrued liabilities	41,000	
Taxes payable	20,500	
Total current liabilities		$165,000
Mortgage note payable		67,000
Total liabilities		232,000
Shareholders' equity:		
Common stock		
(no-par, 12,000 shares outstanding)	140,000	
Retained earnings	238,000	
Total shareholders' equity		378,000
Total liabilities and shareholders' equity		$610,000

Required:

Compute the ratios listed on the following form for Smith's Specialty Stores.

P2. Ratios to be Computed:

Ratio Name	Computation	Answer
Current ratio	_____	___ to 1.0
Liabilities to total equity	_____	_____ %
Shareholders' equity ratio	_____	_____ %
Plant assets to long-term liabilities	_____	___ to 1.0
Turnover of assets	_____	___ times
Return-on-investment	_____	_____ %
Return-on-equity	_____	_____ %
Book value per share	_____	$

Multiple Choice Problems - Solutions

1. b.

2. a. A high P/E ratio indicates the stock market is optimistic about a company's future earning potential. A low ratio indicates concerns.

3. d.

4. d.
    Current assets $250,000
    - Current liabilities 180,000
    Working capital $ 70,000

5. b.
    Total liabilities $480,000
    ÷ Shareholders' equity $270,000

    = 1.78 to 1.0

6. a.
    Current assets $250,000
    ÷ Current liabilities $180,000

    = 1.39 to 1.0

7. c.
    Current assets - (inventory & prepaid insurance) $100,000
    ÷ Current liabilities $180,000

    = 0.56 to 1.0

8. a. First, compute average accounts receivable:
    A/R for 20X2 $ 98,000
    + A/R for 20X1 92,000
    $190,000 ÷ 2 = $95,000 (Average A/R)

    Next, compute accounts receivable turnover:
    Sales $850,000
    ÷ Average A/R $ 95,000

    = 8.95 times

    Finally, compute the number of days to collect accounts receivable:
    Days in a year 365
    A/R turnover 8.95

    = 41 days

9. d. First, compute average inventory:
   Inventory for 20X2 $155,000
   + Inventory for 20X1   164,000
                          $319,000 ÷ 2 = $159,500 (Average inventory)

   Next, compute inventory turnover:
   Cost of goods sold $537,500
   ÷ Average inventory $159,500

   = 3.37 times

   Finally, compute the number of days to sell inventory:
   Days in a year   365
   Inventory turnover   3.37

   = 108 days

10. c. First, compute earnings before interest and taxes (EBIT):
    Net income $ 68,000
    + Bond interest expense   42,000
    + Income taxes   45,000
    EBIT $155,000

    Next, compute times bond interest earned:
    EBIT $155,000
    ÷ Bond interest expense $ 42,000

    = 3.69 times

11. c. Net income $ 68,000
       ÷ Sales $850,000

       = 8.0 %

12. b. Shareholders' equity $300,000
       ÷ Average number of shares outstanding   10,000

       = $30 per share

13. a. Net income $ 68,000
       ÷ Total equity (total assets) $1,000,000

       = 6.8 %

14. b. First, compute earnings available to common shareholders:

Net earnings	$214,000
- Preferred stock dividends	14,000
(2,000 shares x $100 par value x .07 dividend rate)	
Earnings available to common shareholders	$200,000

    Next, compute earnings per share:

Earnings available to common shareholders	$200,000
÷ Average number of shares outstanding	100,000

    = $2 per share

15. b.
Dividend per share	$ 0.75
÷ Market price per share	$37.00

    = 2.0%

16. a.
Market price per share	$37
÷ Earnings per share	$3

    = 12.3 times

Exercise Type Problems

P1. Vertical Analysis

Income Statements

	20X5	20X4
Net sales	100.0 %	100.0 %
Cost of goods sold	79.0	78.0
Gross margin	21.0	22.0
Selling and administrative expenses	9.5	9.0
Operating income	11.5	13.0
Income tax expense	4.2	4.9
Net income	7.3 %	8.1 %

Balance Sheets

	20X5	20X4
ASSETS		
Current assets:		
Cash	6.7 %	13.5 %
Accounts receivable, net	23.4	22.7
Inventory	37.0	36.2
Total current assets	67.1	72.3*
Property, plant, and equipment, net	32.1	26.6
Intangible assets, net	0.8	1.1
Total assets	100.0 %	100.0 %

* error due to rounding

(Continued on the following page.)

P1. Vertical Analysis

Balance Sheet - continued

LIABILITIES AND SHAREHOLDERS' EQUITY		
Current liabilities:		
Accounts payable	29.2 %	27.3 %
Accrued liabilities	14.4	15.8
Taxes payable	1.9	2.1
Total current liabilities	45.5	45.2
Notes payable	1.2	1.5
Bonds payable	13.3	12.0
Total liabilities	60.0	58.7
Shareholders' equity:		
Common stock		
(no-par, 13 shares outstanding)	6.8	8.2
Retained earnings	33.2	33.1
Total shareholders' equity	4.0.0	41.3
Total liabilities and shareholders' equity	100.0 %	100.0 %

P2. Ratios:

Ratio Name	Computation	Answer
Current ratio	$201,500 / $165,000	1.22 to 1.0
Liabilities to total equity	$232,000 / $610,000	38.03 %
Shareholders' equity ratio	$378,000 / $610,000	61.97%
Plant assets to long-term liabilities	$320,500 / $ 67,000	4.78 to 1.0
Turnover of assets	$800,000 / $610,000	1.31 times
Return-on-investment	$ 51,600 / $610,000	8.46 %
Return-on-equity	$ 51,600 / $378,000	13.65%
Book value per share	$378,000 / 12,000 shares	$31.50

Chapter 14
Cash Flow Statement

Learning Objectives for the Chapter

The material in this chapter of the study guide is designed to facilitate your ability to:

- Identify the types of business events that are reported in the three sections of the Cash Flow Statement.
- Convert an accrual account balance to its cash equivalent.
- Prepare a Cash Flow Statement using the T-account method.
- Explain how cash flow from operating activity reported under the indirect method differs from that reported under the direct method.
- Explain how the classifications used on the Cash Flow Statement could provide misleading information to decision makers.

Brief Explanation of the Learning Objectives

Identify the types of business events that are reported in the three sections of the Cash Flow Statement.

There are three sections of the Cash Flow Statement: operating, investing, and financing. The following general rules describe the types of events that usually go in each section. There are exceptions to these rules, but they are beyond the scope of this course.

The *operating section* includes events that typically affect net income; these are mostly related to revenues and expenses. The official pronouncement from the FASB says that anything that is not an investing or financing activity is an operating activity, but the general rule given in the previous sentence usually works.

The *investing section* includes cash activities related to the acquisition and disposal of assets **not** directly related to period expenses (for example, prepaid rent is related to rent expense). Usually, but not always, this means cash activity related to long-term assets is reported as an investing activity.

The *financing section* includes cash flow activity related to obtaining and repaying the financial resources of the business. This includes the borrowing and the repaying of most debt, issuing stock, treasury stock transactions, and the payment of cash dividends. Interest paid on debt goes in the *operating* section.

Significant events that do not involve cash are disclosed in the footnotes to the Cash Flow Statement, **not** on the statement itself. An example would be if a company acquires land by giving the owner a five-year note payable.

Convert an accrual account balance to its cash equivalent.

Usually, revenues and expenses on the income statement do not represent the amount of cash actually received or paid during that accounting period. To convert the accrual-based amounts on the income statement into their cash equivalents usually involves analyzing activity in a related balance sheet account. For example, to determine the amount of cash received due to sales, it is necessary to adjust the *sales* figure appearing on the income statement for the change that occurred in *the accounts receivable* accounts that appear on the current period's and the prior period's balance sheets. This objective is covered in detail with the self-study problems.

Prepare a Cash Flow Statement using the T-account method.

Exercise-type problem P-3 is intended to cover this learning objective.

Explain how cash flow from operating activity reported under the indirect method differs from that reported under the direct method.

Most companies use the ***indirect method*** to report net cash flow from operating activities (CFO). To determine CFO, this method begins with a company's net earnings, or more precisely, its operating earnings, and this amount is adjusted to determine CFO. The adjustments involved are due to business events that affected net earnings, which is an accrual-based measurement, differently than they affected cash flows. Most of the events that cause adjustments relate to items affecting current assets and current liabilities. However, the largest single adjustment usually is due to amortization expense.

The ***direct method***, in essence, determines CFO by preparing a cash-based earnings statement. All cash revenues are listed, and all cash expenses are subtracted from the cash revenues. Rather than refer to cash revenues minus cash expenses as cash net earnings, it is called CFO.

Explain how the classifications used on the Cash Flow Statement could provide misleading information to decision makers.

The Cash Flow Statement is divided into three categories: *operating activities*, *investing activities*, and *financing activities*. The classification of several different events might provide misleading information to decision makers, but the two that follow are common occurrences.

If a company builds a new retail store, the cash spent to acquire the long-term assets (land, building, and equipment) are reported as *investing activities*. However, the cash paid to purchase inventory for the new store is reported as an *operating activity*, even though the new inventory is just as much an investment in the new store as the building itself.

If a company replaces an old machine with a new machine, this cash outflow is reported as an *investing activity*. Thus, the company's Cash Flow Statement gives the impression that the company is expanding when, in fact, its productive capacity is basically unchanged. The Cash Flow Statement does not give readers a way to distinguish cash expenditures that **expand** a company's capacity from those that merely **maintain** its existing capacity.

As noted, this objective has been addressed in almost every previous chapter in the textbook. The articulation problems included in earlier chapters of this study guide also have covered this topic by asking you to show the effects of an event on Net Income and on Cash, among other things. As an example, recall that amortization expense reduces net income but it does not reduce cash.

Self-Study Problems

Matching Problem

Listed below are 20 business events. In the space provided at the end of each description, indicate which section of the Cash Flow Statement, if any, would be affected by that event. If an event involves more than one type of activity, indicate all activities involved. Assume the *indirect method* was used. Use the following letters to indicate your answer:

>   Operating Activities = **O**
>   Investing Activities = **I**
>   Financing Activities = **F**
>   Not on the SCF = **N**

1. The monthly electricity bill was paid with cash.
2. Purchased inventory for cash.
3. Purchased equipment for cash.
4. Issued common stock for cash.
5. Recorded amortization expense.
6. Purchased equipment using a note payable.
7. Issued a term note for cash.
8. Paid cash for three months rent in advance.
9. Recognized that one month's prepaid rent had expired.
10. Paid cash interest on bonds payable.
11. Purchased treasury stock with cash.
12. Sold treasury stock for more that its original cost; received cash.
13. Sold, for cash, an old piece of equipment. The equipment was sold for an amount equal to its book value.
14. Sold, for cash, an old piece of equipment. The equipment was sold for an amount less than its book value (i.e., at a loss).

Matching Problem (continued)

15. Made the annual cash payment for principal and interest on a term loan.
16. Recorded amortization on a patent.
17. Made cash sales.
18. Collected cash from accounts receivable.
19. Paid cash dividends.
20. Issued a stock dividend.

Multiple-Choice Problems

1. Spiceland Co. reported sales of $50,000 in 20X5. Spiceland's balance sheets for 20X4 and 20X5 showed the following:

	20X4	20X5
Accounts Receivable	$10,000	$12,000
Accounts Payable	7,000	10,000

   Based on this information, how much cash did Spiceland collect from sales during 20X5?
   a. $53,000
   b. $52,000
   c. $48,000
   d. $47,000

2. Gourmet Co. reported utilities expense of $15,000 in 20X7. Utilities Payable was $4,000 on January 1, 20X7 and $3,000 on December 31, 20X7. How much cash did Gourmet pay for utilities during 20X7?
   a. $15,000
   b. $16,000
   c. $17,000
   d. $19,000

3. In what sections of the Cash Flow Statement should companies report cash dividends paid and cash dividends received?

	Dividends Paid	Dividends Received
a.	Financing	Operating
b.	Financing	Investing
c.	Operating	Financing
d.	Operating	Operating

4. In what sections of the Cash Flow Statement should companies report cash borrowed with a note payable and interest paid on the note payable?

	Cash Borrowed with Note Payable	Interest Paid on Note Payable
a.	Financing	Financing
b.	Investing	Operating
c.	Financing	Operating
d.	Operating	Financing

5. Which of the following would be a cash inflow from investing activities?
   a. Borrowed cash by issuing bonds payable
   b. Sold inventory for cash
   c. Exchanged land for common stock of another company
   d. Sold used equipment at a loss

6. Cutlery Co. reported $20,000 of rent expense on its 20X3 income statement. The balance in Prepaid Rent was $6,000 on December 31, 20X2 and $4,000 on December 31, 20X3. How much cash did Cutlery Co. pay for rent during 20X3?
   a. $16,000
   b. $18,000
   c. $22,000
   d. $26,000

7. For 20X6 Big-Stoves Co. reported *net income* of $750,000 and *net cash flows from operating activities* of $1,000,000. Which of the following could not have been a reason that Big-Stoves' net cash flows from operating activities were **greater** than its net income?
   a. Amortization expense
   b. Loss on sale of equipment
   c. Decrease in inventory from the beginning of the year to the end of the year
   d. Decrease in wages payable from the beginning of the year to the end of the year

8. Consider the following events that occurred at Grilltop Co. during 20X9:

   Jan. 1 Issued bonds for $100,000.
   Jan. 20 Used cash from the sale of bonds to purchase equipment for $80,000.
   Oct. 1 Sold used equipment for $15,000. This equipment had been acquired in 20X2, and was sold at a $5,000 loss.
   Dec. 31 Paid interest of $8,000 on the bonds.

   Based only on the facts above, what would be Grilltop's *net cash flow from investing activities* for 20X9?
   a. $95,000 decrease
   b. $65,000 decrease
   c. $10.000 increase
   d. $ 5,000 increase

9. On July 1, 20X4, Caterer Co. sold a building for $100,000. The building had cost Caterer $300,000 fifteen years earlier, and had accumulated amortization of $230,000 at the time of sale. What were the effects of this event on Caterer's net income and cash flows?

	Net Income	Cash Flows
a.	$200,000 decrease	$130,000 increase
b.	$ 30,000 increase	$ 70,000 increase
c.	$ 30,000 increase	$100,000 increase
d.	$ 70,000 increase	$100,000 increase

10. The following account balances are available for Fast-Food Co.:

	December 31, 20X5	December 31, 20X6
Equipment	$500,000	$600,000
Accumulated Amortization	200,000	240,000

    During 20X6 Fast-Food Co. sold equipment for $65,000 that had originally cost $80,000. At the time of the sale this equipment had accumulated amortization of $30,000. How much equipment did Fast-Food **purchase** during 20X6?
    a. $110,000
    b. $140,000
    c. $150,000
    d. $180,000

11. In 20X7 the Candy Town Co. had net income of $50,000. Amortization expense for 20X7 was $8,000. Listed below are net changes in selected account balances at Candy Town, for 20X7:

	Net Increase or (Decrease)		Net Increase or (Decrease)
Cash	$(10,000)	Accounts Payable	$(11,000)
Accounts Receivable	13,000	Wages Payable	14,000
Inventory	(12,000)	Long-term Liabilities	12,000
Long-term Assets (net)	15,000		

How much was Candy Town's *net cash flow from operating activities* for 20X7?
a. $60,000
b. $63,000
c. $70,000
d. $73,000

Exercise-Type Problems

P-1 The following account balances are available for the Jamestown Co. for 20X4 and 20X5.

	December 31, 20X4	December 31, 20X5
Accounts Receivable	$70,000	$65,000
Prepaid Rent	10,000	14,000
Wages Payable	18,000	17,000
Interest Payable	12,000	15,000

Also available for 20X5:

Sales	$900,000
Rent Expense	25,000
Wages Expense	107,000
Interest Expense	13,000

Required:

Based on the information above, prepare schedules or T-accounts to answer the following questions:
1. How much cash did Jamestown collect from accounts receivable during 20X5? Assume all sales were initially made on account.

2. How much cash did Jamestown pay for rent during 20X5?
3. How much cash did Jamestown pay for wages during 20X5?
4. How much cash did Jamestown pay for interest during 20X5?

Note: Partially completed schedules and T-accounts are provided for you to use in answering these questions, but you do not need to complete both. Some students understand the T-account method best; others prefer the scheduling technique.

P-1. Forms for Questions.

Schedule for Question 1

Sales $
Beginning Accts. Rec.
Max. that could
 have been collected
Ending Accts. Rec.
Cash collected $

T-Account for Question 1

Accounts Receivable

Beg. Bal. 70,000
Sales
                                    Collected
End. Bal. 65,000

Schedule for Question 2

Rent Expense	$
Ending Prepaid Rent	
Max. that could have been paid	
Beg. Prepaid Rent	
Cash Paid	$

T-Account for Question 2

Prepaid Rent	
Beg. Bal. 10,000	
	Rent Exp.
Cash Paid	
End. Bal. 14,000	

Schedule for Question 3

Wages Expense	$
Beg. Wages Payable	
Max. that could have been paid	
End. Wages Payable	
Cash Paid	$

T-Account for Question 3

Wages Payable	
	18,000 Beg. Bal.
	Wages Exp.
Cash Paid	
	17,000 End. Bal.

Schedule for Question 4

Interest Expense	$
Beg. Interest Payable	
Max. that could have been paid	
End. Interest Payable	
Cash Paid	$

T-Account for Question 4

Interest Payable	
	12,000 Beg. Bal.
	Interest Exp.
Cash Paid	
	15,000 End. Bal.

P-2 This problem is based on the same information presented in problem **P-1** with additional information provided. The information is presented here in a slightly different format; net increases and decreases are given rather than beginning and ending balances. There are several different ways to approach problems related to the Cash Flow Statement. The problems in this study guide deliberately present information in different ways to expose you to different problem-solving styles. Once you determine the way that works best for you, that method can be used to solve most SCF problems.

The following information is available for Jamestown Co. for 20X5:

Account	Net Increase or (Decrease)
Accounts Receivable	$ (5,000)
Inventory	18,000
Prepaid Rent	4,000
Accounts Payable	(5,000)
Wages Payable	(1,000)
Interest Payable	3,000

Net Income for 20X5 was $63,000.
Amortization Expense for 20X5 was $55,000.

Required:

Compute the *Net Cash Flow from Operating Activities* for Jamestown Co. for the year ended December 31, 20X5 using the indirect method. A partially completed schedule is provided below, but you must decide whether to add or subtract each item.

P-2. Form for partial Cash Flow Statement

Jamestown Company
Cash Flow Statement
(Operating Section Only)
For the Year Ended December 31, 20X5

Net Income	$ 63,000
Add or (subtract) the following:	
Decrease in Accounts Receivable	
Increase in Inventory	
Increase in Prepaid Rent	
Decrease in Accounts Payable	
Decrease in Wages Payable	
Increase in Interest Payable	
Amortization Expense	
Net Cash Flow From Operating Activities	$

P-3 *This problem is based on the same information presented in problems **P-1** and **P-2** with additional information provided.*

The following information is available for Jamestown Co. at the end of 20X5:

	December 31, 20X4	December 31, 20X5
Assets:		
Cash	$ 20,000	$ 28,000
Accounts Receivable	70,000	65,000
Inventory	100,000	118,000
Prepaid Rent	10,000	14,000
Equipment	500,000	580,000
Accumulated Amortization	(100,000)	(155,000)
Total Assets	$ 600,000	$ 650,000
Liabilities and Equity:		
Accounts Payable	$ 60,000	$ 55,000
Wages Payable	18,000	17,000
Interest Payable	12,000	15,000
Bonds Payable	150,000	200,000
Common Stock	300,000	300,000
Retained Earnings	60,000	103,000
Treasury Stock	0	(40,000)
Total Liabilities and Equity	$ 600,000	$ 650,000
Sales		$ 900,000
Cost of Goods Sold		637,000
Gross Margin		263,000
Wages Expense	$ 107,000	
Rent Expense	25,000	
Amortization Expense	55,000	
Interest Expense	13,000	200,000
Net Income		$ 63,000

Additional information:
Equipment was purchased during the year for cash. The cost of the equipment was $80,000. Cash dividends of $20,000 were declared and paid. Assume that all sales were made on account and that Accounts Payable relates to inventory purchases.

Required:
Prepare the Cash Flow Statement for Jamestown Co. for the year ended December 31, 20X5. Assume Jamestown uses the direct method. Use the T-account method. Partially completed T-accounts are provided on the following page. A partially completed Cash Flow Statement is also presented on a following page.

P-3. T-accounts for preparing Cash Flow Statement

Cash		Accounts Payable		Common Stock	
Bal 20,000			60,000 Bal.		300,000 Bal.
Operating Activities			55,000 Bal.		300,000 Bal.

Wages Payable		Treasury Stock	
	18,000 Bal.	Bal. 0	
	17,000 Bal.	Bal. 40,000	

Investing Activities

Financing Activities

Interest Payable		Retained Earnings	
	12,000 Bal.		60,000 Bal.
	15,000 Bal.		

Bal. 28,000	

Bonds Payable	
	150,000 Bal.
	200,000 Bal.

Accounts Receivable	
Bal. 70,000	
Bal. 65,000	

	103,000 Bal.

Inventory	
Bal. 100,000	
Bal. 118,000	

Prepaid Rent	
Bal. 10,000	
Bal. 14,000	

Equipment	
Bal. 500,000	
Bal. 580,000	

Accumulated Amortization	
	100,000 Bal.
	155,000 Bal.

P-3. Form for Cash Flow Statement

Jamestown Company
Cash Flow Statement
For the Year Ended December 31, 20X5

Cash Flows from Operating Activities
Cash Receipts from:
    Sales $

Cash Payments for:
    Inventory Purchases $(   )

    Wages   (   )

    Rent   (   )

    Interest   (   )
Total Cash Outflows   (   )
Net Cash Flows from Operating Activities $

Cash Flows from Investing Activities
    Outflow to Purchase Equipment   (   )
Net Cash Flows from Investing Activities   (   )

Cash Flows from Financing Activities
    Inflow from Issuance of Bonds

    Outflow to Purchase Treasury Stock   (   )

    Outflow to Pay Dividends   (   )
Net Cash Flows from Financing Activities   (   )
Net Increase in Cash
    Add: Cash Balance, January 1, 20X4

Cash Balance, December 31, 20X5 $

Matching Problems - Solutions

1. The monthly electricity bill was paid with cash __O__

2. Purchased inventory for cash. __O__

3. Purchased equipment for cash. __I__

4. Issued common stock for cash. __F__

5. Recorded amortization expense. __O__
   Amortization expense is a noncash expense, but it is usually shown as an adjustment to net income in the *operating section* of the SCF. This adjustment is necessary to convert accrual-based net income to cash flows from operating activities.

6. Purchased equipment using a note payable. __N__
   Because the note payable was exchanged directly for the equipment, no cash was involved in this transaction. This noncash transaction would be disclosed in a separate schedule or in the footnotes to the financial statements if its amount is material.

7. Issued a term note for cash. __F__

8. Paid cash for three months rent in advance. __O__

9. Recognized that one month's prepaid rent had expired. __O__
   Recognizing that one month's rent has expired does not involve cash. However, the change in prepaid rent from the beginning of the year to the end of the year is usually shown as an adjustment to net income in the operating section of the SCF. This adjustment is necessary to convert accrual-based net income to cash flows from operating activities.

10. Paid cash interest on bonds payable. __O__

11. Purchased treasury stock with cash. __F__

12. Sold treasury stock for more that its original cost; received cash. __F__
    Purchasing and selling treasury stock is always a financing activity. It does not matter whether the treasury stock was sold for an amount more, less, or equal to its original purchase price.

13. Sold, for cash, an old piece of equipment. The equipment was sold for an amount equal to its book value. __I__

14. Sold, for cash, an old piece of equipment. The equipment was sold for an amount less than its book value (i.e., at a loss). __I, O__
    The cash received from the **sale** of long-term assets, such as equipment, is a cash inflow in the **investing** section of the SCF whether the sale produced a gain, loss, or neither. The **loss** on the sale causes an adjustment to be needed in the **operating** section of the SCF. The loss on the sale reduced net income but did not reduce cash, so an adjustment is necessary to convert net income to cash flows from operating activities.

15. Made the annual cash payment for principal and interest on a term loan. __F, O__
    The portion of the payment on term debt that reduced **principal** would be shown in the **financing** section. The portion that was for **interest** expense would affect **operating** activities.

16. Recorded amortization on a patent. __O__
    Amortization expense, is a noncash expense, but it is usually shown as an adjustment to net income in the operating section of the SCF. This adjustment is necessary to convert accrual-based net income to cash flows from operating activities.

17. Made cash sales. __O__

18. Collected cash from accounts receivable. __O__

19. Paid cash dividends. __F__

20. Issued a stock dividend. __N__
    Stock dividends do not affect cash. This event would be disclosed in the footnotes to the financial statements, however. The same answer would apply if a stock splits had been issued rather than a stock dividend.

Multiple Choice Problems - Solutions

1. c. Sales $50,000
       - Incr. in Acct. Rec.   2,000
       Cash Coll. from Sales   **$48,000**

   OR
   Accounts Receivable

Beg. Bal. 10,000	
Sales 50,000	
	? Collections
End. Bal. 12,000	

2. b. Utilities Expense $15,000
       + Decr. in Utl. Payable   1,000
       Cash Paid for Utilities   **$16,000**

   OR
   Utilities Payable

	4,000 Beg. Bal.
	15,000 Utility. Exp.
Cash Paid ?	
	3,000 End. Bal.

3. a.

4. c.

5. d. Cash received from selling the equipment would be a cash inflow in the *investing* activities section of the SCF. However, the loss on the sale caused net income to decrease, but this loss did not consume cash. Therefore, such losses are usually shown as an adjustment to net income in the *operating section* of the SCF. This adjustment is necessary to convert accrual-based net income to cash flows from operating activities.

6. b. Rent Expense $20,000
       – Decr. in Prepaid Rent   2,000
       Cash Paid for Rent   **$18,000**

   OR
   Prepaid Rent

Beg. Bal. 6,000	
	20,000 Rent Exp.
Cash Paid ?	
End. Bal. 4,000	

7. d.

8. b. Only the events occurring on January 20, and October 20, were investing activities.

Purchase of equipment	$(80,000)
Sale of equipment	15,000
Net decrease from investing activities	**$(65,000)**

9. c.
	Effect on Net Income		
Proceeds from sale			$100,000
less Book value:	Original cost	$300,000	
	Accum. Depr.	230,000	70,000
Gain on sale (increased Net Income)			**$ 30,000**

    The only effect on cash flows was the increase in cash from the proceeds, **$100,000**.

10. d.
Ending Balance in Equipment		$600,000
Beginning Balance in Equipment	$500,000	
- Equipment sold	80,000	420,000
Equipment Purchased		**$180,000**

    OR

    ```
              Equipment
    Beg. Bal. 500,000 |
                      | 80,000  Equip. Sold
    Equip. Pur.   ?   |
    End. Bal. 600,000 |
    ```

11. a.
Net Income	$ 50,000
+ Amortization Expense	8,000
- Increase in Accounts Receivable	(13,000)
+ Decrease in Inventory	12,000
- Decrease in Accounts Payable	(11,000)
+ Increase in Wages Payable	14,000
Net Cash Flow from Operating Activities	**$ 60,000**

Exercise-Type Problems - Solutions

P-1. Solutions for P-1

Schedule for Question 1

Sales	$900,000
+ Beginning Accts. Rec.	70,000
Max. that could have been collected	970,000
- Ending Accts. Rec.	65,000
Cash collected	**$905,000**

T-Account for Question 1

```
        Accounts Receivable
Beg. Bal.  70,000 |
Sales     900,000 |
                  | 905,000  Collected
End. Bal.  65,000 |
```

Schedule for Question 2

Rent Expense	$ 25,000
Ending Prepaid Rent	14,000
Max. that could have been paid	39,000
Beg. Prepaid Rent	10,000
Cash Paid	$ 29,000

Schedule for Question 3

Wages Expense	$107,000
Beg. Wages Payable	18,000
Cash Paid	$108,000
Max. that could have been paid	125,000
End. Wages Payable	17,000

T-Account for Question 2

Prepaid Rent

Beg. Bal.	10,000		
		25,000	Rent Exp.
Cash Paid	29,000		
End. Bal.	14,000		

T-Account for Question 3

Wages Payable

		18,000	Beg. Bal.
		107,000	Wages Exp.
Cash Paid	108,000		
		17,000	End. Bal.

Schedule for Question 4

Interest Expense	$ 13,000
Beg. Interest Payable	12,000
Max. that could have been paid	25,000
End. Interest Payable	15,000
Cash Paid	$ 10,000

T-Account for Question 4

Interest Payable

		12,000	Beg. Bal.
		13,000	Interest Exp.
Cash Paid	10,000		
		15,000	End. Bal.

P-2. Solution for partial Cash Flow Statement

Jamestown Company
Cash Flow Statement
(Operating Section Only)
For the Year Ended December 31, 20X5

Net Income	$ 63,000
Add or (subtract) the following:	
+ Decrease in Accounts Receivable	5,000
− Increase in Inventory	(18,000)
− Increase in Prepaid Rent	(4,000)
− Decrease in Accounts Payable	(5,000)
− Decrease in Wages Payable	(1,000)
+ Increase in Interest Payable	3,000
+ Amortization Expense	55,000
Net Cash Flow From Operating Activities	$ 98,000

P-3. T-accounts for solution

Cash	
Bal. 20,000	
Operating Activities	
(a2) 905,000	660,000 (b3)
	108,000 (d2)
	29,000 (e2)
	10,000 (f2)
Investing Activities	
	80,000 (g1)
Financing Activities	
(h1) 50,000	40,000 (i1)
	20,000 (j1)
Bal. 28,000	

Accounts Receivable	
Bal. 70,000	
(a1) 900,000	**905,000 (a2)**
Bal. 65,000	

Inventory	
Bal. 100,000	
(b2) 655,000	637,000 (b1)
Bal. 118,000	

Prepaid Rent	
Bal. 10,000	
(e2) 29,000	25,000 (e1)
Bal. 14,000	

Equipment	
Bal. 500,000	
(g1) 80,000	
Bal. 580,000	

Accumulated Amortization	
	100,000 Bal.
	55,000 (c1)
	155,000 Bal.

Accounts Payable	
	60,000 Bal.
(b3) 660,000	655,000 (b2)
	55,000 Bal.

Wages Payable	
	18,000 Bal.
(d2) 108,000	107,000 (d1)
	17,000 Bal.

Interest Payable	
	12,000 Bal.
(f2) 10,000	13,000 (f1)
	15,000 Bal.

Bonds Payable	
	150,000 Bal.
	50,000 (h1)
	200,000 Bal.

Common Stock	
	300,000 Bal.
	300,000 Bal.

Treasury Stock	
Bal. 0	
(i1) 40,000	
Bal. 40,000	

Retained Earnings	
	60,000 Bal.
(b1) 637,000	900,000 (a1)
(c1) 55,000	
(d1) 107,000	
(e1) 25,000	
(f1) 13,000	
(j1) 20,000	
	103,000 Bal.

NOTE

Amounts shown in **bold** type were plugged to be the amounts needed to make the T-accounts balance.

P-3. Solution for Cash Flow Statement

Jamestown Company
Cash Flow Statement
For the Year Ended December 31, 20X5

Cash Flows from Operating Activities
Cash Receipts from:
    Sales $905,000

Cash Payments for:
    Inventory Purchases $(660,000)
    Wages   (108,000)
    Rent   (29,000)
    Interest   (10,000)
Total Cash Outflows   (807,000)
Net Cash Flow from Operating Activities $98,000

Cash Flows from Investing Activities
    Outflow to Purchase Equipment   (80,000)
Net Cash Flow from Investing Activities   (80,000)

Cash Flows from Financing Activities
    Inflow from Issuance of Bonds   50,000
    Outflow to Purchase Treasury Stock   (40,000)
    Outflow to Pay Dividends   (20,000)
Net Cash Flow from Financing Activities   (10,000)
Net Increase in Cash   8,000
    Add: Cash Balance, January 1, 20X4   20,000
Cash Balance, December 31, 20X5 $28,000